THE HISTORY OF MI6

THE HISTORY OF MI6

THE INTELLIGENCE AND ESPIONAGE AGENCY OF
THE BRITISH GOVERNMENT

ANTONELLA COLONNA VILASI

authorHOUSE®

AuthorHouse™ UK Ltd.
1663 Liberty Drive
Bloomington, IN 47403 USA
www.authorhouse.co.uk
Phone: 0800.197.4150

© 2013 by ANTONELLA COLONNA VILASI. All rights reserved.

No part of this book may be reproduced, stored in a retrieval system, or transmitted by any means without the written permission of the author.

Published by AuthorHouse   07/01/2013

ISBN: 978-1-4817-9681-1 (sc)
ISBN: 978-1-4817-9682-8 (hc)
ISBN: 978-1-4817-9683-5 (e)

Library of Congress Control Number: 2013911803

Any people depicted in stock imagery provided by Thinkstock are models, and such images are being used for illustrative purposes only.
Certain stock imagery © Thinkstock.

This book is printed on acid-free paper.

Because of the dynamic nature of the Internet, any web addresses or links contained in this book may have changed since publication and may no longer be valid. The views expressed in this work are solely those of the author and do not necessarily reflect the views of the publisher, and the publisher hereby disclaims any responsibility for them.

CONTENTS

Preface vii

Chapter One—On Her Majesty's Service 1
   1.1 Secrets and spies 1
   1.2 The Secret Service Bureau 2
   1.3 Foundation 4
   1.4 In defense of the British Empire 7
   1.5 Before the Great War 8
   1.6 The Foreign Section during World War I 11
   1.7 Interwar era 14
   1.8 World War II 17
   1.9 Cold War 19

Chapter Two—The Modern Day Version 23
   2.1 SIS or MI6: The main threats in the present day 23
   2.2 Skills and Responsibilities of the
       Secret Intelligence Service 30
   2.3 "The Headquarters" 35
   2.4 The British Intelligence Community 37

Chapter Three—The Chiefs of MI6 55
   3.1 Sir George Mansfield Smith-Cumming 55
   3.2 Sir Hugh Sinclair 57
   3.3 Major-General Sir Stewart Menzies 59
   3.4 Sir John Sinclair 61
   3.5 Sir Dick White 63
   3.6 SIR Rennie, John Ogilvy 64
   3.7 Sir Oldfield, Sir Maurice 66
   3.8 Franks, Sir Arthur Temple 67
   3.9 Figures, Sir Colin Frederick 69

3.10 Sir Christopher Keith Curwen 71
3.11 Sir Colin Hugh Verel McColl 72
3.12 Sir David Spedding 73
3.13 Sir Richard Dearlove 75
3.14 Sir John McLeod Scarlett 76
3.15 Sir John Sawers 78

Chapter Four—SIS Special Operations 81
4.1 Cupcake operation 81
4.2 The Falklands Conflict 82
4.3 Jungle operation 83
4.4 The Balkans (1990) 84
4.5 Operation Mass Appeal 85
4.6 Operation Ajax 87
4.7 Pakistan Operation 89
4.8 Operation Victory 91

Conclusions 93

Bibliography 95

Web Sources 97

PREFACE

This account traces the organizational development of MI6 from its foundation in 1909 to the present day. The agency began as the foreign section of the Secret Service Bureau. Both, the Secret Service Bureau, and the subsequent MI6, "remained publicly unacknowledged by the British government for over eighty years and was given a formal legal basis only by the Intelligence Services Act of 1994."[1]

MI6, officially known as SIS, Secret Intelligence Service, is the United Kingdom's foreign intelligence agency. Together with the Security Service or MI5, and the Government Communications Headquarters GCHQ, it forms the heart of Britain's national intelligence community.

The main aim of MI6 is to collect foreign intelligence from human sources on matters of interest to the British government. The agency has also been responsible for carrying out "covert" operations.

These make it analogous to America's Central Intelligence Agency CIA, although MI6 is much older.

Its role stands in contrast to MI5, which collects intelligence on security threats in Britain, and the GCHQ, which monitors electronic communications.

Today, MI6 is based at 85 Vauxhall Cross in London, and is led by Chief John Sawers, a former diplomat who was Britain's ambassador to the United Nations. Its budget and the number of employees are both secrets.

Although most of MI6's history is shrouded in secrecy, it is known to have been part of a number of very important operations since it was first established. Details of MI6 operations and relationships seldom appeared

---

[1] http://www.thenervousbreakdown.com/kjeffery/2011/01/an-excerpt-from-the-secret-history-of-mi6-1909-1949/

in the British press until the 1990, when, for the first time, the secretive organization publicly named its head.

In the first half of the Cold War, the agency collaborated with the American CIA in secret operations to tap communications in East Germany, and the overthrow of the elected government of Iran in 1953, followed by the return of Shah. It was also hit hard by the discovery of a number of high-level Soviet spies in the British government. SIS's current operations are unknown, but it is believed that since the end of the Cold War their focus on Russia and the former Soviet bloc fell; while counterterrorism activity rose substantially. It presumably continues to cooperate with the CIA.

Chapter One

ON HER MAJESTY'S SERVICE

1.1 Secrets and spies

> *"Intelligence agencies have existed in one form or another for centuries; their role was always to spy on each other".*[2]

Intelligence gathering is the process by which nations learn about the military and political activities of other countries, using both overt and covert tactics.

Since society began, nations have tried to protect themselves by learning what was happening inside and outside their borders. Sometime this was done overtly through diplomacy, but sometime the search for valuable information from secretive military and political organizations, has led to the formation of covert intelligence-gathering services around the world.

It can take years to establish a solid network of agents who are able to earn the trust of those they are observing.

Nations have always built secret military intelligence networks with help of *"intelligencers"*[3], *"collectors"*[4] or more commonly *"spies"*: often international business, travelers and politicians. These people can

---

[2] The Spycraft manual by Barry Davis B.E.M pag 3
[3] The British way in cold warfare: intelligence, diplomacy and the bomb by Matthew Grant 2009 pag. 130 Six: The Real James Bonds 1909-1939 by Michael Smith pag. 4
[4] http://www.nationalarchives.gov.uk/spies/spies/default.htm

be very good secret agents because they are often able to gain access to important, valuable or sensitive information from foreign countries.

It is only very recently that official intelligence organizations were founded and spying was considered as a respectable profession. Britain's permanent Secret Service was founded at the beginning of the twentieth century, so it was then that spying started to lose its mark as a dishonest and disreputable way of making a living, a *"shady profession"*[5], and started to become seen as a legitimate way of collecting military intelligence.

1.2 The Secret Service Bureau

British Military Intelligence was born in the early years of the 20th century. In 1909, the War Office in Great Britain authorized the creation of the *"Secret Service Bureau"*.

The Secret Service Bureau was composed of a cluster of military intelligence departments. As time went by, the departments increased or decreased both in size and function, but at their peak they numbered no less than nineteen in total.

They were:

"MI1 - Codes and Cyphers. General code-breaking.
MI2 - Geographic information on other countries.
MI3 - Further geographic information.
MI4 - Aerial Reconnaissance.
MI5 - Security Service, responsible for internal national security.
MI6 - Secret Intelligence Service, responsible for espionage.
MI7 - Propaganda.
MI8 - Communications security and signal-interception. MI-8 was responsible for scanning airwaves for enemy radio-activity.
MI9 - POWs, enemy & allied. POW debriefing, aid to allied POWs, interrogation of enemy POWs (until 1941).
MI10 - Technical analysis.
MI11 - Military Security.

---

[5] A century of spies: Intelligence in the Twentieth century by Jeffry T. Richelson Oxford University Press 1997 pag 3

MI12 - Military Censorship.
MI13 - Section unused.
MI14 - Surveillance of Germany.
MI15 - Aerial defense intelligence.
MI16 - Scientific Intelligence.
MI17 - Secretariat for Director of Military Intelligence.
MI18 - Section unused.
MI19 - Enemy POW (prisoners of war) interrogation".[6]

The Secret Service Bureau was in active duty from the early 1900s through both World Wars and during the Cold War.

Many departments were created as a direct result of the two World Wars, while others were created in response to the Cold War starting in the late 1940s, running to the 1980s.

During this period, some departments altered their function, others even discontinued their activities, though many of them survived decades before ceasing functioning altogether.

MI-6 remains the most famous section of the Secret Service Bureau because of its exposure created by the author Ian Fleming and his world-famous "James Bond" novels and series of films, which continues to this day.

The MI sections began to become defunct in the years during and after the Cold War because many of the MI sections became useless. There were few if any POWs, there was no Germany to fight and there were few, if any, aerial engagements. One by one, the sections were closed down until eventually, only two remained. The two sections that still had a practical use to the British Government outside of an actual military conflict: MI5 and MI6, concentrating on internal national security and on collecting international intelligence respectively.

---

[6] www.informationclearinghouse.info

1.3 Foundation

"The modern Secret Intelligence Service (SIS), known as MI6 (military intelligence 6), the Secret Service" or simply *Six*, is the United Kingdom's external Intelligence Agency.

SIS is responsible for the United Kingdom's espionage activities overseas as opposed to MI5 (*Military Intelligence Section 5*) which deals with internal security.

MI6 is the main British foreign intelligence organization and it is even more secretive than either its American counterpart *(CIA)*, or another member of the British intelligence community, the Security Service or MI5. Although their functions are quite separate, the MI6 and MI5 share origins and their history, in the world wars and Cold War era ran along parallel lines. Yet, whereas MI5 has established a tone of openness with the British public since the early 1990s, MI6 remains guarded concerning the details of its activities.

Before looking at today's system of intelligence in the United Kingdom, it
is very important to first briefly see where the system has come from.

Britain can be seen *"as one of the earliest pioneers of intelligence and espionage"*.[8] The origin of the modern SIS (*Secret Intelligence Service*) goes back at least to the second half of the 15th century, already at that time people charged with acquiring information on behalf of Her Majesty's Government. In fact Sir Thomas Cromwell ran secret agents in Europe on behalf of Henry VIII and Sir Francis Walsingham developed expertise in secret interception, as well as maintaining a network of fifty secret agents abroad while Private secretary to Elisabeth I.

The British navy has long been considered one of the strongest military organizations in the world, reason why until 1909 Britain

---

[7] https://www.sis.gov.uk/
[8] The British way in cold warfare: intelligence, diplomacy and the bomb by Matthew Grant 2009 pag 130
http://www.faqs.org/espionage/Ul-Vo/United-Kingdom-Intelligence-and Security.html#ixzz2BtzMNnbN . . . formerly the Secret Service Bureau Foreign Section gained its present designation MI6 in 1921.

depended primarily on the Naval Intelligence Division (NID) to gather intelligence.

The British *"Secret Service"*, that would eventually become known as **MI6** *(Military Intelligence, section 6)*[9] was set up in 1909 following the threat of Germany's military and naval expansion, with several years of growing concern and panic at the idea of German spies across Britain were planning an attack. Indeed the first SIS assignment was to gather secret information about German military plans.

At the beginning of 1909, a NID mission to photograph a German military harbor failed and two captains were arrested. The scandal led the Royal Navy to take new decisions in reference to its intelligence-gathering abilities, and ultimately to decide that they must create a separate, modernized organization that would be dedicated to gathering military intelligence.

The British Secret Intelligence Service (SIS) was founded as the foreign section of the **Secret Service Bureau** in October 1909. At that time, the Bureau was divided into a naval section and an army section. The naval section was in charge of foreign espionage while the army section was responsible for counterintelligence inside UK. The naval section was turned into MI6 while the army section into MI5.

It was established that the new organization (MI6) *"which must at the same time be in close touch with the Admiralty, the War Office and the Home Office"*[10] had three main objects:

- it served as a screen between the Admiralty, the War Office and foreign spies who may have information that they wish to sell to the Government.
- It had to send agents to various parts of Great Britain, keep in touch with the country police with a view to ascertaining the nature and scope of the espionage that is being carried on by foreign agents; and finally,
- it had to act as an intermediate agent between the Admiralty, the War Office and a permanent foreign agent who should be

---

[9]

[10] Cit. The secret history of MI6 by K. *Jeffry pag. 6*

established abroad, with the view of obtaining information in foreign countries.

Because the Naval Intelligence Division of the Royal Navy conducted early British intelligence gathering, British authorities believed that a naval captain would be the right person to head the first Secret Intelligence Service. *"Royal Navy Chief G. Mansfield Smith-Cumming whose chosen as organization's first head officer on October 1, 1909".*[11]

Commander Mansfield Smith Cumming was fifty years old, an obscure naval officer who had been forcibly retired from the active list owing to chronic sea sickness and had spent the past decade experimenting with the best methods of providing boom defense for Southampton harbor. His office was the center for British intelligence gathering on Germany. In 1914, he was involved in a serious road accident in France, in which his son was killed. *"Legend has it that in order to escape the car wreck he was forced to amputate his own leg using a pen knife"*[12]. Hospital records have shown however that while both his legs were broken, his left foot was only amputated the day after the accident. Later he often told all sorts of fantastic stories as to how he lost his leg, and would shock people by interrupting meetings in his office by suddenly stabbing his artificial leg with a knife, letter opener or fountain pen.

Some Cumming's practices have become British Intelligence traditions. For example *"he initialed papers that crossed his desk in green ink"*.[13] British intelligence officers still do this today. He also often *"dropped the "Smith" and used the abbreviation of Chief "C" as a code name"*.[14] This is the nickname given to all secret chiefs who have followed him.

The new headquarters of the Secret Service Bureau was set up in a second set of offices in Victoria Street under cover of a private detective agency run by a former officer. The Secret Service Bureau,

---

[11] Cit. Inside Britain's MI6 Military intelligence pag. 11
[12] Cit. MI6 The Real James Bond 1909 1939 . . .pag. 8
[13] Cit. Inside Britain's MI6: Military intelligence . . . pag. 10
[14] At her majesty's Secret service. The chiefs of Britain's by Nigel West pag. 21

and the subsequent Secret Intelligence Service, remained publicly unacknowledged by the British government for over eighty years.

1.4 In defense of the British Empire

The need for military intelligence has long been very important to the British.

The United Kingdom has existed as unified nation since the tenth century.

It came into being after the union of England and Wales and it was enacted under *the Statute of Rhuddlan in 1284.*[15]

The Treaty of Union led to a single united kingdom including all Great Britain, in fact, on 1 May 1707 a new Kingdom of Great Britain was created by the political union of the kingdoms of England and Scotland. In the 18th century, the country played a very important role. The British led Industrial, transformed the country and fuelled the growing British Empire. During this time Britain, like other great powers, was involved in colonial exploitation.

The colonies in North America had been the main focus of British colonial activity but with their loss in the American War of Independence, imperial ambition turned elsewhere, particularly to India.

In 1801, while the wars with France still continued, the Parliaments of Great Britain and Ireland each passed an Act of Union, uniting the two kingdoms and creating the United Kingdom of Great Britain and Ireland.

After the defeat of France in the Revolutionary and Napoleonic Wars (1792-1815), the UK emerged as the principal naval and economic power. For most of the nineteenth century, the United Kingdom had been by far the most powerful country in the world, possessing the

---

[15] http://en.wikipedia.org/wiki/Statute_of_Rhuddlan The statute of Ruddlan, also known as the Statutes of Wales or as the Statute of Wales provided the constitutional basis for the government of the Principality of North Wales from 1284 until 1536. The statute was enacted on 3 March 1284 and promulgated on 19 March at Rhuddlan Castle in North Wales after careful consideration of the position by Edward I.

greatest empire ever seen. Britain was described as the *"some gouty giant, with fingers and toes spread across the world "*.[16]

The British Empire grew to include India, large parts of Africa, and many other territories. Alongside the formal control it exerted over its own colonies, Britain's dominant position in world trade meant that it effectively controlled the economies of many countries. By the end of the century, other states began to challenge Britain's dominance. The UK, along with Russia, France and after 1917, the USA, was one of the major powers opposing the German Empire, and its allies in World War I.

1.5 Before the Great War

"C" Cumming laid the foundations of the Service giving its contribution to the First World War in which its networks operating behind German lines in Belgium and France made an important contribution to the Allied victory.

Commander Cumming started his service in a curiously way, he spent his first full day in his office, he wrote in his *"diary"*[17]: *"Went to the office and remained all day, but saw no one, nor was there anything to do"*[18]. Indeed for about a month Cumming had little to do.

Cumming's task was strictly connected with that of three departments overseeing his work: the Foreign Office, the Admiralty and the War Office. During the early months, there was not clear the precise division of responsibilities of the organization and he was disappointed to learn that he was not the chief of the whole Bureau but," *another person, Captain Vernon Kell, "code-name K"*[19] had to work with him and in equal term since he was chosen as head of the home section.

---

[16] The Secret History ok MI6: 1909-1949, Keith Jeffrey, Penguin book 2011 pag 4

[17] The Secret History ok MI6: 1909-1949, Keith Jeffrey, pag 23
The Mansfield Cumming's diary, the most important single source for the early days of the
Secret Service Bureau until the beginning of 1914.

[18] The Secret History ok MI6: 1909-1949, Keith Jeffrey, pag 3

[19] Cit The secret history of MI6 by K. Jeffry pag 8

THE HISTORY OF MI6

By the end of 1909, despite various difficulties and restrictions, such as economic, organizational and the problems arising from the secrecy of the service; Captain Cumming with Captain Kell who together, had been appointed to run a Secret Service Bureau, were able successfully to establish an embryonic organization devoted to the clandestine collection of foreign intelligence.

Already in a first stage, Cumming was thinking sensibly about the problems of foreign intelligence work, but much of this was ambitiously optimistic, and would remain so for years. Even thirty years after, in the Second World War, after substantial advances in wireless technology, establishing reliable and secure agent communications from behind enemy lines proved very difficult indeed.

So after a slow and not very easy start the work increased and the Chief described the various agents in a report to the committee overseeing the Secret Service Bureau.

They split into several types:

Those who "*are not required to collect definite information or send in periodical reports, but who are expected to keep a good look out for any unusual or significant movements or changes either Naval or Military and report them*". From these agents "*no news is good news*" *and in the absence of any evidence to the contrary, it is to be believed that they are doing their duty and are earning the pay they receive. It has been pointed out that this negative news is of great value and that although we may wait for years for any report, it may be invaluable when it comes. On the other hand this class of agent should be very carefully chosen and should be of proved character, as very much will depend upon them, and the temptation will be strong when the critical moment arrives, to avoid risk by doing nothing.*

The second kind:" *those who in addition to giving warning of extraordinary activity on the part of those they are deputed to watch, are expected to collect information of all kinds and forward it to me at stated intervals—I cannot as yet speak with any authority, as sufficient time has not elapsed since their appointment to enable me to form an opinion"*[20].

He then added a third group, which given the straitened circumstances of the British secret service for most of its existence was to become an important supplement to its agent networks. There was in

---

[20] Cit MI6 The real James Bond by M. Smith . . . pag 18

fact another source of intelligence besides Cumming's various agents. It came from army and navy officers looking for adventure.

The most productive of Cumming's agents were a small group of men in shipping or arms industries who either regularly traveled to or resided in Germany and combined their business travels with part-time intelligence work. Much of that intelligence work did not involve actual espionage. Instead, Cumming's part-timers collected a wide assortment of newspapers and journals published in Kiel, Whilhemshaven, Danzig and Berlin. They also observed the harbors and waterfronts of Hamburg and Bremen, homes to major shipyards, and of Kiel.

The most successful of Cumming's known networks was run by Max Shultz, a naturalized Southampton ship-dealer.

Four informants, the most important being an engineer named Hipsich, in Bremen's Weser shipyards. In the two years Hipsich operated before being detected he had the opportunity to inform the British about Germany's battleship plans and apparently handed over a large collection of drawings.

Cumming's German networks provided an abundance of technical intelligence on the German navy.

In addition to Germany, Rotterdam, Brussels and S. Petersburg were targets of Cumming's spies. Richard Tinsly, code name T, headed Cumming's operations in Rotterdam. Tinsly had developed a successful shipping business, which he used as a cover for his intelligence work. But a future permanent undersecretary at the Foreign Office, found T *"a liar and a first-class intriguer with few scruples"*.[21]

Cumming's Belgian network was both larger and more disreputable than the Dutch network. Henry dale Long, code name L, served as a chief of operations in Brussels from 1910. However, the Brussels network did business with a free-lance Brussels intelligence service, that sometimes sold fabricated intelligence including false German invasion plans.

Cumming was also persuaded in purchasing an alleged German codebook which a wartime cryptanalyst later showed to be without importance.

---

[21] Cit. A Century of Spies: Intelligence in the Twentieth century by T. Jeffry pag 33

Cumming's ability to find and recruit really good agents was obstructed in part by rivalry for control of what agents could be found between the admiralty, the war office, Kelly's Home Section and himself and in another part by his limited access to UK government facilities abroad.

The foreign Office's determination to retain exclusive control of political intelligence proposal, also meant that Cumming was forbidden access to members of the consular service abroad. This proved a major obstacle, as consular officers would naturally have had the best access to both British and foreign nationals whom Cumming might have recruited as agents. Despite these limitations, Cumming's Foreign Sections achieved a surprising degree of success, especially in terms of German war preparations.

1.6 The Foreign Section during World War I

The organization's first significant test of the service came with the First World War, during which it had mixed success. SIS was unable to penetrate Germany itself, but had some significant successes in military and commercial intelligence; this was achieved mostly by means of agent networks in neutral countries, occupied territories, and Russia. The First World War, which lasted a four year period between 1914 and 1918, erupted as a result of the complicated European alliance system. The assassination of Austrian Archduke Ferdinand, and his wife, Sophie, by Serbian nationalists sparked the conflict, when Russia backed by France declared their intent to defend Serbia, should Austria declare war. The Austrian government, with its ally Germany declared war on Serbia three days later. British forces joined the French and Russians and the United States, resolved to remain out of the conflict. During the first World War, Cumming's relationship with each of the three departments he was serving, inevitably changed in August 1914 with the service ministries' growing demands for immediate operational intelligence. This was especially true of the War Office because the staffing of British Military Intelligence was immediately affected by the outbreak of war.

Problems of status and hierarchy continued, no one was very clear who precisely was in charge of the Secret Service.

In those years Cumming suffered a serious car accident, he was severely injured resulting enforced immobility and the Secret Service was reorganized, the Secret Service was brought more closely under War Office control. *"Lord Oratio Herbert Kitchener[22] reorganized the British War Office in 1915, returning the Secret Intelligence service to its control"*[23]. The British Imperial Security Intelligence service (MO5) was renamed MI5. For separate units were organized: MI1x for organization and administration, MI1a for operational intelligence, MI1b for censorship and propaganda, and *"MI1c for secret service and security"*.[24]

During the World War I, there were several changes, the science of cryptography assumed a distinctly modern character. New developments, such as the international telegraph system and the telephone left cryptologists dealing with new ways to adapt encryption methods to the new technology. The ultimate goal of cryptologists of the era was to invent a means of transcribing and decoding ciphers without the use of bulky codebooks that could easily fall into enemy hands. War time experimentation proved impractical, so for most of the war, both sides relied on older style codebooks. Since codes were becoming more and more intricate and complex, intelligent services recruited language translator and professional 'code brakers': the cryptologists.

The ruinous loss of four of the Germans's codebooks proved extremely favourable for the British troops, whose cryptologists unit, called Room Forty, deciphered a considerable amount of German codes over the warefare period. *"The department was founded under the direction of intelligence officer Reginald Blinker and the code expert Alfred Ewing, it was located in Room 40 of the Admiralty Building"*.[25]

---

[22] http://www.britannica.com/EBchecked/topic/319651/Horatio-Herbert-Kitchener-1st-Earl Kitchener/3937/Additional-Reading
In World War I, Herbert Kitchener, British field marshal and secretary of state for war, assembled and organized one of the mightiest armies in his country's history.

[23] Cit MI6 Inside Britain's military intelligence 6 by Shaun McCormack pag 16

[24] http://www.britannica.com/EBchecked/topic/379632/MI6 During the first World War, Cumming's organization was known as MI1(c).

[25] http://www.faqs.org/espionage/Ul-Vo/United-Kingdom-Intelligence-and-Security.html

THE HISTORY OF MI6

The cryptology department housed in Room 40 was only a small branch of Britain's large intelligence system.

It was responsible for a series of important naval decrypts at the Battle of Jutland in May/June 1916 which were largely misused by the Admiralty and, rather more spectacularly, in deciphering the Zimmermann Telegram in 1917, which suggested a German plot to assist Mexico is annexing United States territory. The latter helped to bring the United States into the war on the side against the Central Powers. Room 40 also played a notable role in securing the capture of British traitors and Irish patriots.

The Great War ended on November 11, 1918. In the postwar period the foreign section was considered unable to employ full time agents and was forced to fold in casual agents, agents whose performance was unsatisfactory.

Whether or not SIS was guilty of genuinely failing to produce adequate intelligence, is a recurrent problem in evaluating the agency's work throughout its history. In times of real crisis, the demand for intelligence is potentially unlimited, and no volume can be sufficient.

Although just five years old when the war began, the organization had already established intelligence station in Holland, France and Egypt. SIS had effectively combated counterespionage, interrogate prisoners, gathered information from behind enemy lines, and organized escape routes for fleeing prisoners of war. SIS was not without productive sources such as the Belgian "***White Lady or Dame Blanche***"[26]: an extraordinary network of men, women and indeed children, who were operating in occupied Belgium and France in World War I, obtaining information about German troop movements, weaponry and so forth, and reporting directly to the British secret service. They were so effective that during the last 18 months of the war, la Dame Blanche was said to be supplying more than 75 percent of the intelligence coming out of occupied Belgium and France.

"***Train watchers***"[27]: a network that could monitor the movements of almost every military troop. They recorded troop movements from behind enemy lines. People travelled mostly by train in those days,

---

[26] Cit The Secret History of MI6 By K, Jeffry . . .pag 78
[27] Cit MI6:The Machinery of Spyng . . . pag 46

aviation was in its early stages and trains were the fastest way to move soldiers from place to place. Agents passed military intelligence back into allied territory with trained carrier pigeons. Another important figure of the period is represented by the well placed and reliable German marine engineer Herman Krueger known by his Dutch station controllers by the symbol TR 16 or simply as The Dane.

1.7 Interwar era

Intelligence did not disappear from the international scene after the end of World War I, even if economic resources were significantly reduced and that meant, that for almost two decades the Service had to operate in financial straits; at a time when the new revolutionary regime in Soviet Russia appeared to pose a major threat. After the end of hostilities, the debate over the future structure of British Intelligence continued at length but Cumming managed to engineer the return of the Service to Foreign Office control.

At this time, the organization was known in *"Whitehall"*[28] by a variety of titles including the *"Foreign Intelligence Service"*, the *"Secret Service"*, *"MI1(c)"*, the *"Special Intelligence Service"* and even *"C's organization"*. Around 1920, it began increasingly to be referred to as the Secret Intelligence Service (SIS), a title that it has continued to use to the present day and which was enshrined in statute in the Intelligence Services Act 1994.

If the time before the first world war was the period that led to the creation of the Secret Intelligence Service (SIS), it was the interwar period in which it most developed the features of a truly modern Secret Service. It was during this interval that the agency acquired that distinctive internal tasking and the diffusion of the official history term the *"1921 arrangement"*, which remains almost unique to the agency ninety years later. *"It was trough the 1921 arrangement that SIS first acquired the*

---

[28] http://en.wikipedia.org/wiki/Whitehall_Court
It was used as Secret Intelligence Service (MI6) headquarters until the end of World War I.

nick-name MI6".[29] As result, the years from 1921 to 1939 are the crucial period for understanding the fundamental relationship between SIS and its masters and its essential status and function within the machinery of British central Government. After the war SIS, precisely during the 1920, created a close operational relationship with the diplomatic service. It established the post of ***"Passport Control Officer"***[30] within embassies, based on a system developed during World War I by British Army Intelligence. This provided operatives with a degree of cover and diplomatic immunity but had become compromised by the 1930s. At the same time was introduced also a central foreign counter-espionage **"Circulating Sections"**[31] to give greater control on its objectives to its consumer departments, mainly the War Office and Admiralty. The Circulating Sections enacted the intelligence requirements that the operational group sections had to meet and restored the intelligence to the consumer departments. This pact was called the "1921 arrangement" and the structure of internal structure of the agency is still grounded on this rule.

Immediately after World War I and throughout the 1920s, the SIS, led by Sir Mansfield Smith-Cumming, focused its attention on Communism and Russian Bolshevism. "*Smith-Cumming died, in his office, in 1923 and was replaced as "C" by Admiral Sir Hugh Sinclair*".[32] He had joined the Royal Navy in 1886 and while lacking the charisma of his predecessor, he had a clear vision for the future of the agency which developed a range of new activities under his leadership.

Chief Sinclair started espionage activities inside Russia. The agency also tried to bring down the Communist Party with the help of people like **Boris Savinkov**, "*a Russian writer and revolutionary terrorist who collaborated with the British Secret Service. He was involved in a number of counter—revolutionary plots against the Bolsheviks*"[33] And **Sidney Reilly** "*a Russian-born adventurer who worked for British Secret Intelligence Service*

---

[29] Mi6 and the Machinery of Spying: Structure and Process in Britain's Secret . . . Di Philip H. J. Davies Pag 17
[30] Cit MI6 and the Machinery of Spying . . . pag 64
[31] Cit MI6 The Machinery of Spying . . . pag 79
[32] Cit Inside Britain's military Intelligence 6 . . . pag 16
[33] http://www.spymuseum.com/pages/agent-reilly-sidney3.html

for a time. His legend grew after his death and Ian Fleming used him as a model for James Bond".[34] He began to work for MI1c, forerunner of MI6, was briefly trained and sent to Russia. After a successful mission he received British citizenship to become an official agent. Later he adopted the Irish surname "Reilly", which was the surname of his first wife's father.

In 1922, MI6 took charge of the Government Code & Cypher School (GC&CS), formed from the remains of the British Admiralty's Room 40, along with a smaller War Office program. GC&CS soon proved successful at breaking ciphers used by the new Bolshevik government. MI6 efforts against both Russia and Germany in the 1930s uncovered evidence of Nazi-Soviet cooperation in the development of weapons technology, but during this era, MI6 also suffered a number of failures, leaving the British government unprepared for such moves as Hitler's reoccupation of the Rhineland in 1935. Unfortunately Sinclair had inherited an organization in financial turmoil. The reduced peacetime budget forced him to cut back and close down intelligence stations. It is generally accepted that Sinclair focused too heavily on the rise of the communism in Russia. This created a reduced espionage activity in and against Germany which gave the Nazi regime more freedom to grow without being watched. The new director of MI6 Sinclair endowed the agency with new responsibilities. He started Circulation Section "Section V" that worked in collaboration with MI5 to perform counterintelligence. This partnership sought to gather information from counter intelligence in many countries. Such information would then be handed to M16 agents in every corner of the world. Over this time, other sections were created. These included:

- Section N, for the interception of foreign diplomatic mail;
- Section D, for paramilitary actions in wars (covert political actions), which would later become, during the World War II, the Special Operation Executive (SOE);
- Section 7, for the economic espionage;
- Section 8, for the radio communications of SIS operatives.

---

[34] http://www.spymuseum.com/pages/agent-reilly-sidney3.html

THE HISTORY OF MI6

Sinclair died in 1939, after an illness and was replaced as "C" by Lt. Col. Stewart Menzies, *"code name Horse Guards"*[35], who had been with the service since the end of WWI.

1.8 World War II

World War II began on September 1, 1939, when German invaded Poland. In return, Britain and France declared war on Germany two days before.

This is a not very easy period for SIS organization. *"The most significant failure of the service during the war is an incident, at Venlo in the Netherlands in 1939"*[36], unfortunately seven years of operations were thrown away. The officers leading the two supposedly separate groups were ordered to meet a representative of an anti Nazi group, together. The Germans turned out to Abwehr officers and captured the SIS officials and within months had rolled up both networks.

When finally German invaded France in 1940 there were disastrous effects on British Intelligence. Czechoslovakia, Austria and Poland had already fallen to the Germans. Norway, Denmark, Holland, Belgium and the Balkans were on their way down. SIS was left with few neutral positions in Europe from which to run its intelligence efforts, apart Sweden, Switzerland and Portugal SIS was blind to continental events.

British Prime Minister Winston Churchill formed his war cabinet on May 10, 1940, which had strong feelings about the supervision and operations of Britain's secret intelligence organizations and the human intelligence work of the service was overshadowed by several other initiatives. For MI6 a new era began, just three months after the outbreak of war, Colonel Stewart Menzies became the new "C." Fortunately for SIS, the new 'C' Stewart Menzies was to make extraordinary use of both his friendship with the Prime Minister Churchill and the steady flow of Ultra decrypts of the German Enigma traffic.

So it was that MI6 began to direct its efforts to decipher intercepted military transmissions by the enemy in Europe and Asia. Most of the

---

[35] Cit At her majesty's secret service . . . pag 49
[36] Cit The Secret History of MI6 . . . pag 382

enemy codes were produced on the German Enigma cryptographic machine.

Enigma was an encoding system devised by the Germans in 1926 and employed also by many other nations during Warld War II and after. It was the very first automated device used worldwide able to chypher messages. The messages it produced were so confusing and tangled that both the Germans and their enemies thought it was unbraekable. However, Polish and British mathematicians finally cracked the system in time to allow the Allies to access German military communications for the duration of World War II. The site of cracking, for what the Great Britain is concerned, was centered at the "Code and Cipher School at Bletchly Park"[37] near London.

Without this kind of operations, SIS may well have been disbanded and replaced by its wartime rival, SOE. "*SOE*"[38] was Special Operations Executive, formed on July 19, 1940 and closed on January 15, 1946, when many of its agents moved to MI6. It was created to coordinate subversion and sabotage in enemy occupied countries. SOE agents distributed propaganda, blew up bridges, directed air strikes, destroyed factories, and taught resistance tactics.

After the fall of the France the organization received the authorization to begin operations to divert German, Italian, and Japanese attention away from the main fighting fronts towards the rear areas.

Such division, whose headquarters were disseminated in London, was formed by three sections: SO1 devoted to propaganda, SO2 for active operations, and SO3 for planning. By 1944 SIS did not heal enough and was still not able to be a major intelligence agency without the material coming from Bletchley Park. "C" Menzies masterly deployed all his political and social acquaintances to gain time to allow the survival of SIS. In 1946 his strategies proved successful when he convinced the Labour Government to terminate SEO activities and relocate its best

---

[37] http://www.faqs.org/espionage/Ul-Vo/Ultra-Operation.html The codename for the British cryptologists efforts at Bletchley Park to intercept and break German coded messages was "Operation Utra"

[38] http://it.wikipedia.org/wiki/Special_Operations_Executive

minds and projects to SIS. Because of this 'restyling', GC & CS became a brand-new organization called "GCHQ"[39]

This cause the Foreign Office to leave SIS orphan of its main source of intelligence. Altough partially mutilated, SIS was sill being controlled by the Foreign Office and kept its name.

1.9 Cold War

After the end of World war II, Berlin was divided in four sectors. The Russian, Americans, British and French, each controlled a portion of the city although the Russian controlled the largest part which covered most of eastern Berlin. The citizens of Berlin traveled freely between all the sectors until 1952, when the borders were closed between east and west Germany.

In 1961after a disastrous summit between American president Kennedy and Soviet Premier Khrshchev, the east Germany government built the wall that completely surrounded west Berlin.

Communist Russia began to extend its influence over eastern Europe and north Korea during the 1950s. This led the United States and communist Russia to become involved in what is known as the *Cold War*. A constant state of nonviolent hostility, the Cold War apparently ended with the collapse of Soviet Russia in 1991.

After World War II, MI6 returned its focus to espionage in the Soviet Union. By the end of 1950, MI6 was convinced that the Soviet Union was intent on war.

The British MI6 and the American Central Intelligence Agency (CIA) were linked together in a number of operations, both nations were bent on stopping the spread of Communism in Europe, believing that it threatened the existence of democracy. The support and funding of different groups such as exiles and students provided a powerful anticommunist propaganda machine.

---

[39] http://www.gchq.gov.uk/Pages/homepage.aspxGCHQ was originally established after the First World War as the Government Code and Cypher School (GC&CS or GCCS), by which name it was known until 1946. During the Second World War it was located at Bletchley Park.

The American CIA which also trying to prevent the spread of Communism, was much wealthier than MI6. British intelligence officers cooperated with the CIA in projects to investigate European anticommunist spy networks.

Intelligence agents were also involved in anticommunist groups aimed at teens. For example the European Youth Coalition (EYC) that was born in 1950s and flourished in the 1960s. Its purpose was to undermine Soviet efforts to influence political opinion of the young.

The 1960 were both the best and the worst time for MI6 involvement with American CIA. Several intelligence gathering accomplishments drew admiration of the United States. This was good for MI6 because the CIA could provide them with financing and technology that MI6 could not afford on its own. But this was overshadowed by continue mole hunts to determine the names and duties of counterintelligence agents within MI6 and revealed its inner workings to the United States.

Beginning in 1958 MI6 had three undercover agents working inside Uzard Bezpieczenstwa (UB), the Polish secret intelligence service. The most noted agent was code name **Noddy**. Poland's close relationship with the Russian KGB meant that MI6 could watch the inner workings of the Russian Intelligence gathering of Noddy and the other two agents. MI6 passed KGB information to CIA' official: the most valuable intelligence ever collected.

"*Double agents Oleg Penkovsky and George Black created tremendous problems for MI6 and CIA at this time*"[40]. Penkovsky was a high ranking Soviet official who worked for both MI6 and CIA. Blake worked for MI6 and funneled information to the KGB. Black blew the cover on hundreds of western agents when he provided detailed information to Soviet Intelligence KGB about the MI6 and CIA. The CIA feared that Blacke's confession to KGB might blow the cover on Penkovsky's operations. Penkovsky was a double agent for Britain. As a Soviet agent he had access to Soviet Intelligence which he funneled to MI6. When he was finally caught, it was great loss. Thanks to Penkovsky, the agency was able to recruit several reliable sources within the USSR. He provided the agency several thousand important documents about the Russian

---

[40] Cit Inside Britain's military Intelligence . . . pag 29

military. He was able to provide Russian rocket manuals that uncovered Soviet plans to deploy missiles in Cuba.

Penkovsky was arrested on October 22 by the KGB and then

SIS activities included a range of covert political action successes, including the overthrow of Mohammed Mossadeq in Iran in 1953, while in the early 1960s, the Intelligence community was also concerned about events in Vietnam. MI6 supported the United States.

Budget cutbacks and cold war concentration in the 1970s put MI6 into a delicate position, the MI6's attentions were towards Russian yet and when Michail Gorbachev was elected to head the Soviet Union, Crakdov believed it was a subversive political plot to trick the world to thinking the Soviets were beginning to back down from the threat of starting World War III. This mindset prevented MI6 to understand the true political tides in Eastern Europe and Soviet Union. So when East German borders guards began breaking down the Berlin wall on November 10, 1989, MI6 was shocked and surprised. The fall of the Berlin wall was a symbolic end to the Soviet Empire.

During the 1980s and 1990s, MI6 recovered its standing through successful operations in the Falklands War, Persian Gulf War, and Balkan wars. It gained new statutory grounding with the 1994 passage of the Intelligence Services Act, which defined its responsibilities and functions, as well as those of its chief. The act also set in place a framework of government oversight for MI6 activities. In 1993, Sir Colin McColl became the first MI6 director. He was replaced in 1994 by Sir David Spedding, and in 1999, Spedding was replaced by Sir Richard B. Dearlove.

CHAPTER TWO

THE MODERN DAY VERSION

2.1 SIS or MI6: The main threats in the present day

Since 1920, the organization began increasingly to be referred to as the *Secret Intelligence Service (SIS)*, a title that it has continued to use to the present day.

"MI6" has become an alternative title for SIS, especially in the minds of those outside the Service. It was used extensively during the Second World War and although it fell into official disuse years ago, *"many writers and journalists continue to use it to describe SIS"*[41].

After the fall of the Berlin wall, in 1989, SIS shifts its focus to the intelligence challenges which are dominant such as: the proliferation of weapons of mass destruction, cyber security, terrorism and international crime.

In February 1999, Richard Billing Dearlove was selected by British foreign secretary Robin Cook and Prime Minister Tony Blair from a short list of candidates drawn from inside and outside the MI6.

"Dearlove's election as the new "C" was made public, it was only the second time MI6 had ever made a "C" public appointment even if no photograph was released".[42]

"Dearlove was born in Cornwall and was educated at Monkton Combe School, he joined MI6 when he was twenty-one years old and before assuming

---

[41] https://www.sis.gov.uk/our-history/sis-or-mi6.html
[42] http://ews.bbc.co.uk/2/hi/uk_news/politics/286128.stm

the role of "C" he worked as MI6's assistant Chief".[43] British newspapers reported that Dearlove's appointment reflected a new commitment in the post Cold War era to combat international organized crime as well as MI6's more traditional espionage activities.

The advancement of Communism in Russia, the major concern for MI6, had faded away since the end of the Cold War. It had begun after World War II when the British and American with the Soviet Union alliance began disintegrate. While the Soviet sought to expand communism in Europe and beyond, the British and Americans feared this was a threat to democracy. In turn the Soviet were concerned about the spread of democracy throughout the world. Each side built up its military arsenals including nuclear weaponry, as the possibility of a war between them.

During this period, which lasted until a collapse of the Soviet Union in 1991, MI6 worked closely with America's CIA to stop the spread of Communism in Eastern Europe and to learn about Russia's nuclear missile technology.

"The last Known confrontation between MI6 and Russia came in 1991when one British spy and four British diplomats were thrown out Russia. MI6 spy Rosemary Sharpe was accused of paying three German intelligence agents for information about Russian military equipment. The German agents failed to pass the money to their superiors and were investigate for corruption. The investigation blew the covers on Sharpe and another British spy". [44]

MI6 pays its employees based on performance. The more information they gather, the more money they make.

This is done to motivate agents to uncover valuable intelligence. Agent who fail to achieve MI6 goals can be fired.

Like other intelligence agencies acquires some information by setting up fake companies or political groups called *"front groups"*. [45]

---

[43] Cit At her majesty's Secret service. The chiefs of Britain's by Nigel West pag 243

[44] Cit Inside Britain's MI6 By S. Mckormack.... pag 36

[45] http://www.sourcewatch.org/index.php/Front_groups A front group is an organization that purports to represent one agenda while in reality it serves some other party or interest whose sponsorship is hidden or rarely

THE HISTORY OF MI6

Front groups give MI6 the ability to put agents in places where they can gather valuable information. In this case, front means fake. People in front groups wear friendly masks to hide their true agendas.

Front groups function in the same way that an individual agent does. Members must spend time establishing their covers.

The MI6 is often involved in uncovering information on terrorist activities and plots.

In recent years, Northern Ireland and Irish Republican Army (IRA) have been key targets of MI6 intelligence gathering operations. Several attacks in London were linked to the IRA from July 2000 to November 2001.[46]

A Russian built Mark 22 anti-tank weapon attacked MI6 spy headquarters in central London in September 2000. A missile from the rocket launcher shattered an eight floor window of the MI6 building. British authorities suspected that the IRA was responsible for the bombing. Like most of the world's intelligence agencies, MI6 now focuses its efforts on terrorist networks throughout the world as a result of the terrorist attacks on the World Trade Center in New York and on the Pentagon outside Washington, D.C., on September 11, 2001. British intelligence reported in February 2001 that top members of Osama Bin laden's al Qaeda terrorist network, the organization accused the terrorist

---

mentioned. Intelligence agencies use front organizations to provide "cover", plausible occupations and means of income, for their covert agents.

[46] http://news.bbc.co.uk/2/hi/events/northern_ireland/paramilitaries/69824. stm 1 June 2000: A bomb exploded on Hammersmith Bridge at 4.30 am.

September 2000, The Real IRA, a group which had split from the Provisional IRA, launch an RPG-22 at the MI6 building in central London, causing damage.

4 March 2001 BBC bombing: At around 00:30 GMT, the Real IRA detonated a car bomb outside the BBC's main news centre in the Shepherd's Bush area of west London.

6 May 2001: A bomb exploded at a Royal Mail sorting office in Colindale, London at 01.53 GMT, injuring one person. This bomb came just three weeks after an almost identical blast at the same office.

3 August 2001 Ealing bombing: The Real IRA detonated a car bomb in Ealing Broadway, West London, injuring seven.

attack in the United States, were hiding in Lebanon. MI6 believes that Hezbollah terrorist network was assisting twenty or more senior Al Qaeda members. *"The Hezbollah was held responsible for the 1983 attack that killed 241 U.S marines in Beirut"*.[47]

Musa Kusa, the head of Libyan leader Moammar Gadafi's External Security Organization, met with MI6 officials in February 2001. He identified more than a dozen Libyans living in the U.K. who have links to bin Laden's Al Qaeda network.

Over the next several years, as a worldwide intelligence community is committed with global terrorist organizations, it appears that technical intelligence gathering will move toward the internet.

Stories in newspapers and on television about secret intelligence information have been posted on the world wide web: in May of 1999, Government were desperately trying to shut down a web site where dozens of MI6 agents had been identified. Several agents were uncovered. MI6 officials feared that the web site had the potential to damage its worldwide operations. The web site, based in the United States, revealed the name of 117 people including a lot who were not MI6 agents.

A second web site identified nine MI6 agents named in a court document signed by Richard Tomlinson, a former MI6 officer. Tomlinson claimed that the agency was involved in a scandal that was responsible for *"the death of Princess Diana"*.[48] He received a flurry of e-mails and letters after his name was connected to the court document used in the list.

The list of 117 names appeared on a web site related to the Executive Intelligence Review, a publication that prints idea about the Government conspiracy theories.

The list included the names of current MI6 chief Richard Dearlove, former chief Sir David Spedding and former MI6 middle east controller Geoffrey Tantum. It included names of MI6 officers stationed in sensitive areas like the Balkans, where Tomlison served as an MI6 agent. MI6 was especially concerned about the safety of agents in unstable areas because it would become harder to ensure their safety.

---

[47] http://www.masters-table.org/forinfo/hezbollahviolenceTimeline.htm
[48] Princess Diana the Hidden evidence by J. King J. Beveridge Roundhouse publishing 2001 pag 51

THE HISTORY OF MI6

Foreign secretary Robin Cook said not all the name on the list were connected with MI6 *"Nevertheless the released of any such list, however inaccurate it may be, is a deeply irresponsible and dangerous act".*[49]

This security breach showed how dangerous the internet can be as an intelligence weapon. But many people believe that within the next few years, little information on the web will be considered top secret, because the web itself its becoming more of a mainstream outlet for information.

This is why British officials tried to pass legislation that will allow them to monitor internet traffic.[50] By doing this, they are able to track known agents as they surf the web. In most cases, MI6 is able to block the posting of sensitive intelligence information before it is discovered.

Tomlinson has told the British media that he believed the internet will mean the end of the intelligence services.

Over the next several years, the value of information distributed on the web will change. Society as a whole will change. As more and more people become wired for the web, sensitive intelligence quickly becomes common knowledge. As society becomes more and more dependent on the internet, MI6 and other intelligence services will probably rely more on human intelligence than on the advanced technology to conduct espionage. They especially don't want secret intelligence information printed in mass media outlets.

Over the first decade of our century, the energies are also spent on trying to locate terrorist networks and pursuit their future actions. It is for this reason that MI6, as well as other agencies, will focus on infiltrating these groups and stop their activities.

The intelligent staff required to such operations is large in number and competences. Since terrorism gained momentum, information about terrorist organizations gathered by the intelligence has been either overlooked or ignored altoghether, as have been a large amount of small military or terrorist groups. This happens because large intelligence agencies constantly underestimate security threats from such groups, which are considered weak and minor.

---

[49] http:/ /news.bbc.co.uk/2/hi/uk_news/343039.stm
[50] The Regulation of Investigatory Powers Act (RIPA) approved in the year 2000

The lack of prestige and reliability of the intelligence in the United Kingdom is due to poor collaborative efforts between MI5 and MI6.

Power struggles and different policies are the main reasons of these organizations's failures.

"The terrorist attacks in the United States on September 11, 2001",[51] are a milestone of failure in the history of the U.S.A. America was suddenly woke up with the death of thousands of innocent people: these attacks proved America and the whole world that a small group of terrorists could success in their dangerous aim when organized and equipped with intelligence information. The underestimation of intelligence was fatal: intelligence information was sent to the American Government well before the attacks in New York City and Washington D.C., but these were utterly overlooked and considered weak and vague.

On the other hand, Al Qaeda intelligence might have been able to intrude into America's Airlines' security system and monitor timetables, schedules and flight paths. Not only. Al Qaeda succeeded in finding out architectural features of the World Trade Center's Twin Towers and utilize them to identify weaknesses in the structure. By putting together heterogenous pieces of intelligence information, Al Qaeda militants performed one of the most shocking terrorist act in the history of humanity.

Apart from the horror they caused on the entire world, paralyzing and terrorizing not only the people but also the global economy, these terrorist attacks revealed the desperate and firm need for better intelligence cooperation and information-gathering.

How was this all possible? Al Qaeda had been present and active both in the U.K. and the U.S. for several years befor the 9/11 attacks. Starting with its foundation in 1988, the organization had performed, during the 1990s, military operations in Asia, the Middle East, Africa, Europe,

---

[51] http://www.britannica.com/EBchecked/topic/762320/September-11-attacks
Also called 9/11 attacks, series of airline hijackings and suicide attacks committed by 19 militants associated with the Islamic extremist group al-Queda against targets in the United States, the deadliest terrorist attacks on American soil in U.S. history. The attacks against New York City and Washington D. C., caused extensive death and destruction and triggered an enormous U.S. effort to combat terrorism.

THE HISTORY OF MI6

virtually in every continent, and now in America too. It is for this global dimension of the organization that the intelligence community thinks Al Qaeda is dealing with other terrorist groups all over the world. The global scale of the phenomenon requires a collaborative effort between intelligence services: satellites and spy planes are believed to be insufficient in order to gather important information about this terrorist organization: to intercept phone calls or any other communication (such as e-mails and faxes) within Al Qaeda might not be enough if one wants to reveal sensitive information, since the terrorist networks are aware of the risks they take and already have succeeded in avoiding eing detected by such technologies.

Most military information transmitted over the web or wireless communication networks is sent using encryption, which blocks access to data. Encryption changes words into a slew of mixed symbols, numbers, and letters. Ideally, only the sender and recipient of the encrypted messages have the tools to decode information. Most of the world's digital data spying tools are unable to read encrypted message.

In the coming years, national intelligence organizations will focus on developing better human intelligence, although it will be very difficult to place operatives in key locations. Al Qaeda officials were stationed when they launched the September 11 attack. The intelligence community is concerned that it is nearly impossible for a British or American undercover agent to blend into the culture of the region.

One alternative is to work with Pakistan's Inner-service intelligence (ISI) organization which has agents who understand Afghanistan's culture and speak *"Pushtu"*.[52] But there are fears that Al Qaeda has already infiltrated ISI. If ISI has been thoroughly infiltrated by Al Qaeda, MI6 will end up revealing more intelligence than it gathers by working with Pakistani agency.

"The death of Osama Bin Laden (The founder and the spiritual leader of the organization) at the hands of U.S. Navy commandos on May 2011 was a setback to al-Qaeda, but the Islamic terror organization remains a potent threat around the world".[53]

---

[52] Native language of Pakistan.
[53] http:/ /usatoday30.usatoday.com/news/world/story/2012-04-29/bin-laden-anniversary/54630274/1

2.2 Skills and Responsibilities of the Secret Intelligence Service

Oversight of SIS and its operations is exercised through Ministers (primarily the Foreign Secretary), Parliament (The Intelligence and Security Committee) and two independent Commissioners who provide judicial expertise. The arrangements are set out in two key pieces of UK legislation:

"the Intelligence Services Act 1994" and the *"Regulation of Investigatory Powers Act 2000"*.

<u>The Intelligence Services Act 1994</u> *"is largely modeled on the Security Service "Act of 1989"*[54] *which dealt with the Security Service (MI5). That Act substantially followed the structure of "the Interception of Communications Act 1985"*.[55]

The new Act, the 1994 Act, deals with both the Secret Intelligence Service (SIS) and the Government Communications Headquarters (GCHQ) and, most importantly, it establishes for the first time a system of parliamentary accountability for all three service".[56]

The 1994 Intelligence Services Act allows SIS to gain and give information regarding the acts and intentions of overseas people and directs SIS to perform other tasks, enabling the Service to conduct covert operations and to act clandestinely overseas in support of British Government objectives.

The Act placed SIS and GCHQ on a statutory footing for the first time.

---

[54] Public Law Mark Elliott, Robert Thomas, Oxford University Press, pag 407
"The Security Service act 1989 established legal framework only for the Security Service".

[55] Cit. Public Law Mark Elliott, Robert Thomas, pag 406
"The Interception of Communications Act 1985 allowed communications (telephone, fax, telex and post) to be intercepted when authorized by warrant signed by a Secretary of State for highlighted reasons.

[56] John Wadham "The Intelligence service act 1994" The Modern Law Review Limited 1994 Vol. 57, Issue 6 pag 916

An Act

- to make plans on the Secret Intelligence Service and the Government Communications Headquarters, including permissions to fulfil certain actions and the ways in which such authorizations are to be kept under scrutiny;
- to make further plans about authorizations issued by the Security Service; to rule the investigation of complaints about the Secret Intelligence Service and the Government Communications Headquarters;
- to make plans for the institution of an Intelligence and Security Commitee which aim is to keep under scrutiny all three bodies and for related purposes.

According to what the act says the role of an MI6 agent was defined as: "*to obtain and provide information relating to the actions or intentions of persons outside the British Islands; and to perform other tasks relating to the actions or intentions of such persons*" [*in relation to*] *the interests of national security, with particular reference to defense and foreign policies . . . the interests of the economic well-being of the UK . . . or in support of the prevention or detection of serious crime.*[57]

The Act instituted a tribunal to investigate complaints and a committee (the Intelligence and Security Committee) composed of nine members of the parliament reporting to the Prime Minister. The Act also established that the Secretary of State for Foreign and Commonwealth Affairs had the power to grant immunity from British prosecution to SIS personnel when they engage in any acts while on operations abroad that would be illegal under British law, such as murder.

"The Regulation of Investigatory Powers Act 2000" (RIPA) received Royal Assent in July 2000. The aim of the Act is to warrant that the investigations of the intelligence service, police and the military are used in full respect of human rights.

The Act was allegedly introduced to keep pace with technological changes such as the growth of the Internet and strong encodement. The Act provides a basis for authorization and use by organizations of

---

[57] http://www.mi5.com/security/mi6org/index.htm

surveillance and regulates the techniques employed and safeguards the public from invasions of privacy.

"*The act:*

- enable the government to demand that an "ISP"[58] provides access to a customer's communications in secret;
- enable mass surveillance of communication in transit;
- enables the government to demand ISPs fit equipment to facilitate surveillance;
- enable the government to demand that someone hands over keys to protected information;
- *allows the government to monitor people's internet activities;*
- *prevents the existence of interception warrants and any data collected with them from being revealed in court."*[59]

Thus SIS is appointed by the British Government to gather intelligence around the world in order to keep the Nation secure, to prevent attacks and to defend its foreign and economic policies. Therefore, it is not independent on what the intelligent requirements are concerned, but it striclty depends on the Government wich keeps under scrutiny and classifies such requirements. The aim of SIS is to collect secret information and organize covert intelligence and military operations overseas in accordance with the British Government needs and targets and under the priorities set up by the Joint Intelligence Committee and approved by the Ministers of the Government. In order to meet these standards, SIS employs both persons and technologies and establishes a cooperation with other foreign intelligence and security services, as well as working side-by-side with all the other British intelligence agencies: uses human and technical sources to meet these requirements, as well as liaison with a wide range of foreign intelligence and security services and also works closely with the other British intelligence and security agencies: the Security Service and GCHQ, the Armed Forces, the Ministry of Defense, the Foreign and Commonwealth Office, the Home Office and HM Revenue and Customs. The main role

---

[58] ISP: Internet service Provider

[59] http://www.magnacartaplus.org/bills/rip/index.htm

THE HISTORY OF MI6

of SIS is that of *countering terrorism, combating weapons proliferation, supporting stability overseas and securing the UK's cyber advantage.*

—Terrorism has become the first and foremost issue for the National Security Risk Assessment. Al Qaeda, based in the areas of Afghanistan and Pakistan and with a moltitude of supporters and associated groups all over the world, has been assessed the principal terrorist threat to the U.K. and its affairs abroad. Such threat has diversified over the last years, as more and more groups affiliated to Al Qaeda have developed independence in directing their operations. Altough terrorism cannot be erased altogether, risks can be controlled and reduced. With this respect, the U.K. has committed itself in the international collaboration against the threat. Since 2003, the U.K. has been executing a long-term policy to oppose and limit the damages of both terrorism and extremism with the aim of countering the risk of international terrorism and let the citizens live their lives without fear. Such strategy of counter-terrorism is called "*CONTEST*"[60] and divides its aim in four main activities:

1. "*Prevent - to stop people becoming terrorists or supporting violent extremism*
2. *Pursue - to stop terrorist attacks*
3. *Protect - to strengthen our protection against terrorist attack*
4. *Prepare - where an attack cannot be stopped, to mitigate its impact*".[61]
5. The role of SIS is to discover and unsettle terrorist threats. An essential part of the process is the partnerships and collaborative efforts with the other British agencies and departments, as well as other allied countries' partner agencies all over the world. It is for this reason that SIS works in cooperation with the Security

---

[60] http://www.homeoffice.gov.uk/publications/counter-terrorism/counter-terrorism-strategy/
Counter-terrorism strategy (CONTEST). The aim of CONTEST is to reduce the risk to the UK and its interests overseas from terrorism, so that people can go about their lives freely and with confidence. The scope of this revised CONTEST strategy has been broadened to cover all forms of terrorism. Our counter-terrorism strategy will continue to be organised around four work- streams, each comprising a number of key objectives.

[61] http://www.cornwall.gov.uk/default.aspx?page=28753

Service. Agents of the SIS are employed to provide important intelligence on the terrorists' goals and plans.

—The British Government works to reinforce the international non-proliferation pact, and to prevent other states from developing and spreading Chemical, Biological, Radiological and Nuclear Weapons (CBRN).

The U.K. Government also strives to discover efforts by proliferator states to acquire CBRN weapons and the ways in which these weapons are delivered. This includes that the Government also controls exports rigorously in order to prevent terrorist states and groups to have access to such weapons.

SIS's role is pivotal in the Government's Counter Proliferation programme, as it provides secret intelligence on the covert activities of such proliferator states and strives to disrupt such activities.

—One of the principal risks to national security comes now through the cyber space and the internet, as well as other telecommunication networks. Such risks include a failure in the U.K.'s cyber infrastructure and the actions of cyber criminals. The role of SIS in this issue is that of providing the Government with plans and organizations of such governmental and personal cyber threats against the state. The National Security Strategy believes that political instabilities and conflict overseas can contribute in creating a fertile ground for the developing of organized terrorism. An eye must always be kept on those weak and conflict-affected countries: instability and political weakness mean a lack of internal security and this readily undermines the country's development. Well-timed interventions, mainly political, can prevent the possibility of a long-term instability and a more economically burdensome remedy. The duty of SIS is that of providing useful information and warnings on potentially hostile actors and their means, whether be it a state or a non-state. Another SIS's role is that of providing strategic understanding and influence politics and decision-making through the gathering of as much information as possible. By means of its secret agents, SIS also passes secret information to advocate the U.K. government in its institutional work in opposing terrorism.

"MI6's work is divided in two main sections:
Directors of production on a geographical basis:

DP1: covers Europe. There is a Controller for the Northern Area (P1) covering the Soviet Union and Scandinavia; a Controller for the Western Area (P2) responsible for France, Spain and Northern Africa; and Controller for the Eastern Area (P3) covering Germany, Austria and Switzerland.
DP2: Controller for the Middle East (called P4)
DP3: Controller for Far East (P5) which also covers Latin America.
DP4: responsible for London-based operations".[62]

It's important to note that because of the secrecy of the operations and the particular nature of secret service's work, it is not easy to get information, comment and details on operations, staff, agents, or relations with foreign intelligence services, reason why SIS does not even have a Press Office.

2.3 *"The Headquarters"*[63]

Since 1995 SIS headquarters has been at 85 Vauxhall Cross, on the South Bank of the Thames.[64] Over time, several seats were occupied by the organization, it's first accommodation, from 1909 until 1909 was at 64 *Victoria Street*. The Secret Intelligence Service's modest origins as the Foreign Section of the Secret Service Bureau were reflected in the austerity of its first quarters. Both the Foreign and the Home Sections of the Bureau took up office space at 64 Victoria Street, Westminster, rented from an enquiry agent.

---

[62] http:/ /archive.is/HyDm
[63] https:/ /www.sis.gov.uk/our-history/buildings.html
[64] Secret Places, Hidden Sanctuaries: Uncovering Mysterious Sites, Symbols, and societies by Stephen Klimczuk, Gerald Warner Sterling publication 2009 pag 21

Then SIS moved in *Ashley Mansions* from 1909 till 1911

Those were the days of "C" Mansfield Cumming, the first Chief, he worked long hours and most weekends. He wished to find an accommodation that would combine both an office and living quarters. Ashley Mansions in Vauxhall Bridge Road, Westminster was his choice. From 1911 to 1919 *Flat 54, 2, Whitehall Court*, Westminster.

It brought several advantages, not least a greater proximity to the War Office, Admiralty and Foreign Office in Whitehall, as well as more space for the expanding Service. It remained headquarters until the end of the First World War.

During the period from 1919 to 1926 it was the turn of *Melbury Road*.

As result of security issues and reductions in the Service's finances and personnel then led to a move away from Westminster to West Kensington.1, Melbury Road combined the function of office and residence of the Chief of SIS. *"It was here that Cumming died in June 1923"*.[65]

Broadway Buildings, 1926-1964

A need to return nearer to the seat of government prompted yet another relocation. By 1926 SIS had moved into Broadway Buildings, 54, Broadway, near to St James's Park Underground Station. At first, SIS and its recent adjunct, the Government Code and Cypher School (GC&CS), occupied only the fourth and fifth floors but with the outbreak of the Second World War the whole building was taken over and GC&CS moved to Bletchley Park.

Century House, 1964-1994

SIS remained at Broadway for almost forty years until in 1964 it moved to Century House, a modern tower block in Westminster Bridge Road, Lambeth. This was the Service's home for thirty years during the latter half of the Cold War. And finally *Vauxhall Cross* from 1994 to present.

---

[65] The Routledge Companion to UK Counter-Terrorism by Andrew Staniforth, Fraser Sampson pag 33

In 1995 SIS moved to its present headquarters, Vauxhall Cross. Although almost within sight of its first headquarters, the large and prominent building on the banks of the River Thames is very far from the Service's humble beginnings in Victoria.

The building was designed by Sir Terry Farrell and built by John Laing. MI5 was seeking alternative accommodation and co-location of the two services was studied. In the end this proposal was abandoned due to the lack of buildings of adequate size and the security considerations of providing a single target for attacks. In December 1987 Prime Minister Margaret Thatcher's Government approved the purchase of the new building for the SIS.

The building design was reviewed to incorporate the necessary protection for Britain's foreign intelligence gathering agency. This includes overall increased security, extensive computer suites, technical areas, bomb blast protection, emergency back-up systems and protection against electronic eavesdropping.

"On the evening of 20 September 2000, the building was attacked using a Russian-built RPG-22 anti-tank rocket. Striking the eighth floor, the missile caused only superficial damage. The Anti-Terrorist branch of the Metropolitan Police attributed responsibility to the Real IRA." [66]

2.4 The British Intelligence Community

MI6, the Secret Intelligence Service, is with MI5, the Security Service, the best-known component of the British intelligence structure, but this is just a part of a vast intelligence apparatus.

Command and control operates through no less than four entities:

- *the Central Intelligence Machinery*
- *the Ministerial Committee on the Intelligence Services*
- *the Permanent Secretaries' Committee on the Intelligence Services and the*
- *Joint Intelligence Committee.*[67]

---

[66] Cit The Routledge Companion to UK CounterTerrorism by Andrew Staniforth, Fraser Sampson pag33
[67] http://www.fas.org/irp/world/uk/

MI5, or the Security Service, responsible for internal national security.

The Government Communications Headquarters (GCHQ) is in charge of the Communications intelligence is the responsibility of The Government Communications Headquarters (GCHQ), and operates side-by-side with the Communications Electronics Security Group, while other agencies deal with their own itelligence through the Ministry of Defense. Scotland Yard, that is, London Metropolitan Police, also has its department of intelligence, called the Special Branch.

The institution which vigilates over the British Intelligence is the Central Intelligence Machinery, dependent directly on the Prime Minister's Cabinet Office. The Intelligence Community and committees in both houses of the Congress coordinate both intelligence and security agencies. The Central Intelligence Machinery is in charge to assess, observe and relate on the activities and results of every agency, as well as deciding and distributing the resources.

Altough the Central Intelligence Machinery leads all operations, there is another institution which exerts external control upon all intelligence activities: the Ministerial Committee on the Intelligence Services. It is through this institution that the Prime Minister, assisted by the Secretary of the Cabinet, presides day by day over the whole British intelligence and security systems. The distribution of roles and authorities is as follows: The National Criminal Intelligence Service, Scotland Yard and MI5 are controlled by the Home Secretary, while GCHQ and MI6 are supervised by the Foreign and Commonwealth Secretary.

Ministers are advised and assisted in their task by the Permanent Secretaries' Committee on the Intelligence Services. Lastly, the Joint Intelligence Committee (JIC) provides National Intelligence Estimates. JIC makes sure that GCHQ and MI6 fulfil the requirements of the general intelligence scopes and standards.

"The UK's intelligence network consists of five agencies of which the main three—MI5, MI6 and GCHQ".[68]

In short, *MI6 operates under the formal direction of the Joint Intelligence Committee (JIC) alongside the internal Security Service (MI5),*

---

[68] http:/ /www.globalsecurity.org/intell/world/uk/cim.htm

the Government Communications Headquarters (GCHQ) and the Defense Intelligence (DI).[69]

2.4.1 MI5-Security Service

MI5 is closely related with the birth of MI6. In March 1909, the Prime Minister, Mr Asquith, instructed the Committee of Imperial Defense to consider the dangers from German espionage to British naval ports. On 1 October, following the Committee's recommendation, Captain Vernon Kell of the South Staffordshire Regiment and Captain Mansfield Cumming of the Royal Navy jointly established the Secret Service Bureau. To fulfill the Admiralty's requirement for information about Germany's new navy, Kell (K) and Cumming (C) had different role. 'K' was in charge of the counter-espionage on the British land, while 'C' was in charge of the intelligence overseas. Between March 1909 and the outbreak of the First World War, more than 30 spies were identified by the Secret Service Bureau and arrested, thereby depriving the German.

During that period the Secret Service Bureau staff counted only ten people, Kell included and quickly became a division of the War Office, since January 1916, when it merged with the newborn Directorate of Military Intelligence with the name of MI5.

"Wartime legislation increased the responsibilities of MI5 to include the coordination of government policy concerning aliens, vetting and other security measures at munitions factories. MI5 also began to oversee counter-espionage measures throughout the Empire. By the end of the War, during which a further 35 spies were identified and arrested, MI5 had approximately 850 staff." [70]

A detailed history of the work and activities of MI5 during World War I is written in the surviving records of the Agency, published in November 1997 by the Public Record Office. The Bolshevik takeover in October 1917 marked the beginning of a new era for MI5, as it now

---

[69] http://www.ovguide.com/secret-intelligence-service
[70] Espionage: Spies and Secrets by Richard M. Bennet, James Bamford, Virgin 2003, pag 337

began to investigate on the threats of Communist insurrection within the military and the perils of sabotage of military actions.

The MI5 was formally passed responsibility for the evaluation and handling of all threats to the national security on 15 October 1931, with the exception of those coming from anarchism and Irish terrorism. *"This date marked the formation of the Security Service, although the title MI5 has remained in popular use to this day".* [71]

After Hitler's takeover a new menace needed to be faced by the Service, coming from Fascists subversion. But at the beginning of World War II MI5 was not prepared to confront its many and diverse tasks. Such duties included:

- counter-espionage;
- keeping under surveillance enemy aliens and counselling on emprisonment;
- appraising vetting inspections for government departments;
- examining companies engaged with the war in order to instruct them on security measures aimed at opposing sabotage and espionage;
- evaluating reports by common people with respect to suspicious activities.

By early 1939 the Service counted only 30 officers, and only 6 of them were appointed in the surveillance section. Moreover, the German bombing of September 1940 destroyed a great amount of the Service's records.

Just before the beginning of the War, MI5 had moved to Wormwood Scrubs Prison; by the end the following year, in late 1940, the staff were fled and relocated to Blenheim Palace. Months later, in early 1941, Sir David Petrie was nominated the first Director General of the Security Service, and was granted the financial and structural resources to re-organize its Agency.

All the German agents were imprisoned at the outbreak of the War, depriving the enemy of its more powerful weapon. Once the War ended,

---

[71] Espionage: Spies and Secrets by Richard M. Bennett, James Bamford, Virgin 2003, pag 337

in 1945, the German intelligence records disclosed that all the other 200 agents thought to have escaped the British forces had been in fact all identified and seized. "*Some of these agents were turned by the Service and became double agents who fed false information to the Germans concerning military strategy throughout the War. This was the famous "Double Cross" system*".[72]

This proved highly successful and contributed to the remarkable achievement of the Allied Forces in Normandy on *"D Day"* in June 1944.[73]

After the War, in 1952, Prime Minister Winston Churchill delegated his authority over the Security Service to the Home Secretary, Sir David Maxwell Fyfe, who established the new Service's duties and took the role of Director General. The new Directive laid the foundations of the Service's activity until 1989, when the Service had its first statute granted by the Security Service Act.

The consequences of the Sir Fyfe's moves were soon to be seen: by the mid-1950s the Service's officers and staff counted 850 members, including 40 Security Liaison Officers overseas who assisted and advised Commonwealth governments. After Nazi Germany was vanquished and a new post-war era took over, the Cold War, focus of the Service's intelligence turned once again to the Soviet Union and Communism. During the War the Communist Party of Great Britain counted no less than 55,000 members, so the attention towards this issue never really quietened down, but it was in 1948 that the anti-authoritarianism wave reached its peak, when Prime Minister Clement Attlee declared "vital

---

[72] Cit Espionage: Spies and Secrets by Richard M. Bennett, James Bamford pag 338

[73] http:/ /www.army.mil/d-day/ June 6, 1944, 160,000 Allied troops landed along a 50-mile stretch of heavily-fortified French coastline to fight Nazi Germany on the beaches of Normandy, France. General Dwight D. Eisenhower called the operation a crusade in which "we will accept nothing less than full victory." More than 5,000 Ships and 13,000 aircraft supported the D-Day invasion, and by day's end on June 6, the Allies gained a foot- hold in Normandy. The D-Day cost was high -more than 9,000 Allied Soldiers were killed or wounded -- but more than 100,000 Soldiers began the march across Europe to defeat Hitler.

to the security of the state" the exclusion of both Communists and Fascists people from work, achieved by the Service through a scrupolous screening system of espionage all over the country.

"*The cases of Philby, Burgess and MacLean, in particular, showed how effective the Russian Intelligence Service had been before the War in recruiting ideologically-motivated spies in Britain*".[74](Ho tolto il giallo perchè è una citazione)

During the 1960s a considerable number of agents and spies were detected in the U.K., underlying the relevance of the counter-espionage and the need to improve efforts and resources in this direction. These spies included: the Portland spy ring, George Blake, ofFicer of SIS, and John Vassall, who worked at the Admiralty and was also a spy for the KGB. Another goal of the Service's activities during this period was the Profumo Affair of 1963, where the intelligence's role was publicly disclosed by Lord Denning's report. The height of the anti-Communism campaign culminated with the exclusion of 105 Russian personnel from work and their expulsion from the country in 1971, to the great detriment of Soviet intelligence work in London.

A shift on focus marked the late 1970s, when intelligence resources were displaced and directed towards Foreign affairs: Irish terrorism and international terrorism. The growth of Palestinian terrorism in the late 1960s had already been a focus of interest for the Service. In the early 1980s a series of terrorist attacks tested the Service's means and collaboration with other agencies and its fundamental role in the coordination with other Western intelligence services, particularly in two major occasions: the terrorist encirclement at the Iranian Embassy in London (1980) and at the Lybian People's Bureau (1984).

Another major goal for the Service came in 1983 when spy Michael Bettaney, an agent of the Service was found guilty of passing information to the KGB and later convicted of espionage. This led the Security Commision inquiry, who was severe with certain methods of the Service, to appoint Sir Antony Duff as Director General. His leading role in the Service was marked by the discussion he started on the role of the Service, which led to the strengthening of the prestigious and legal

---

[74] Cit Espionage: Spies and Secrets by Richard M. Bennett, James Bamford pag 339

status granted by the Security Service Act in 1989. In other words, his leadership was the base for the structure of the Service as we know it today.

By the early 1990s, the end of the Cold War and the defeat of the Communist regimes, the Service's attentions shifted once again: subversion and espionage were suddenly minor threats and required less of the Service's resources. Irish terrorism was now the agenda. The intelligence responsibility to fight against such terroristic attacks on the British land was transferred to the Service in October 1992. The Service profited from the experience acquired during the fight against other types of terrorism during the past two decades, so much so that the joint efforts of Service and police departments resulted in 18 acquittals for terrorism between 1992 and 1998.

A large number of planned terrorist attacks were impeded, including bombings in large cities. During the 1990s the Service has had other significant improvements thanks to the cooperation with other agencies and departments, particularly for what the weapons of mass destruction are concerned. In 1996 the 1989 Act was revised and expanded to grant the Service the permission to support the police with further means in the seizing and prevention of crime and in 1994 the Intelligence and Security Committee was founded thanks to the new Intelligence Service Act, which implemented the Security Service Act by giving the Service further external surveillance powers.

In the meantime, transparency measures have been established in order to give the public more information on the Service while, on the other side, keeping the secrecy of its operations and avoiding damaging or or risking the lives of its agents. The first transparency move was the publication of a booklet with and address for public correspondence in it, published in 1993 and reissued in 1996.

Second came a series of public speeches given by the Director General Stella Rimington, such as the Dimbleby Lecture of 1994. Then, in 1997, the Public Record Office was published containing the Service's early history. Finally, the recruitment of staff employed in general assignments was openly advertised in magazines and newspapers.

"The Security Service operates under the statutory authority of the Secretary of State (the Home Secretary), but it is not part of the Home Office".[75] In every democracy, we might say, there is a contradiction between espionage of a Security Service with its intrusiveness and the need to preserve one's own privacy. In order to keep the majority safe, the Service may require to spy on the lives of a minority, to prevent covert threats to the state, but there must be rules and surveillance. In order to do so, the Service is the object of constant external oversight with the following responsibility precautions:

- *The Director General is accountable under the Security Service Act 1989 to the Home Secretary. He is appointed by the Home Secretary in consultation with the Prime Minister and is required to submit a report to them annually. The Director General is statutorily responsible for all aspects of the operations and efficiency of the Service, and for ensuring that it obtains and discloses information only in accordance with its functions under the Act.*
- *The Security Service Act that provides for an independent Tribunal, supported by a Commissioner (a senior judge), to investigate complaints about the Service from members of the public. The Commissioner is also responsible for reviewing the issue by the Secretary of State of Property Warrants under the Intelligence Services Act 1994.*
- *The Interception of Communications Act 1985 also provides for a Tribunal, supported by a Commissioner (also a senior judge), to investigate complaints about interception of telephone or postal communications. The Commissioner is also responsible for reviewing the issue of interception warrants by the Secretary of State.*
- *Under the Intelligence Services Act 1994, the Service, together with SIS and GCHQ, is overseen by the Intelligence and Security Committee, a committee of Parliamentarians, on matters of expenditure, administration and policy.*

---

[75] The New Home Office by Bryan Gibson published by Waterside Press 2007, pag 87

- *The Service's performance, plans and priorities are subject to external scrutiny and validation by a senior Whitehall committee, known as SO (SSPP), reporting to Ministers.*

The Director General has one Deputy who is responsible for overseeing intelligence operations. There are five branches, each headed by a Director: three branches are engaged in intelligence investigations and in advising on protective measures to counter the various threats; the other two are responsible for intelligence collection, production and information management, and for personnel, security, finance and facilities management. There is also a Legal Advisers department. In addition, the Service fills the post of Director and Coordinator of Intelligence (Northern Ireland), who reports separately both to the Director General and to the Secretary of State for Northern Ireland.

The Director General, Deputy Director General, the Directors and the Legal Adviser meet regularly as the Management Board of the Service to consider policy and strategic issues. In particular, the Management Board decides how the priorities and organization of the Service should change to reflect shifts in the pattern and intensity of threats."[76]

The Service currently employs several people, who are mostly based at its headquarters at Millbank in central London. The Director General has a Deputy who oversees intelligence operations, and there are six Directors. The Service is divided into branches, each headed by a Director.

"*Senior Management*
- *Director general*
- *Deputy Director general*
- *Director and Coordinator of Intelligence (responsible for Northern Ireland)*
- *Legal Adviser*

---

[76] MI5: The Security Service, Third Edition. See: http://cryptome.org/jya/mi5.htm

Departments
A Branch Operational Support
6A1A: Technical operations, covert entry, eavesdropping devices, CCTV coverage of premises

- *A1F: As above, but on longer-term targets like embassies and head*
- *A2A: Transcription of intercept material*
- *A3 and A5: Technical support for operations. This includes specialized covert phtotography and lockpickers to assist in covert entries.*
- *A4: Mobile and static surveillance units*

B Branch Human Resources

- *B1: Protective security for MI5, including security of building and vetting of MI5 staff*
- *B2: Personnel*
- *B7: Training and recruitment*

D Branch—Non-Terrorist Organizations

- *D1: Vetting of people outside MI5*
- *D4: Counter-espionage, notably on Russia and China*
- *D5: Agent runners for this branch*
- *D7: Organised crime*

G Branch—International Terrorism

- *G2P: Counter-proliferation*
- *G3A: Co-ordination of threat assessments*
- *G3C: Countering terrorism in other parts of the world not covered elsewhere by G Branch*
- *G6: Agent running for G Branch*
- *G9A: Countering threats from Libya, Iraq, Palestinian and Kurdish groups*
- *G9B: Countering threats from Iranian state terrorism and Iranian dissident groups*
- *G9C: Countering Islamic extremists*

H Branch—Corporate Affairs

- *H1 and H2: Liaison with Whithall and the media. Covert financial enquiries with financial institutions. This section liaises with the*

police, policy, custom, ports and immigration. It's also responsible for management policy, including information technology.
- *H4: Finance*
- *The following sections are also part of H Branch*
- *R2: Main registry*
- *R5: Y-boxed files. These are files with restricted access within the Service.*
- *R10: Registry for temporary files*
- *R20: Responsible for administering GCHQ material*

T Branch—Irish Terrorism
- *T2A: Investigates Republican and Loyalist terrorism on the British mainland*
- *T2B: Liaises with local Special Branches and agent runners*
- *T2C: Assesses threats from Irish terrorist groups*
- *T2D: Researches Irish terrorist groups*
- *T2E: Liaises with Metropolitan Police Special Branch, based at Scotland Yard*
- *T5B: Investigates arms trafficking*
- *T5C: Counters Irish terrorism in continental Europe, including the Republic of Ireland*
- *T5D: Counters Irish terrorism in the rest of the world*
- *T5E: Studies terrorist logistics*
- *T8: Runs agent for T Branch; includes a section based in Northern Ireland".*[77]

2.4.2 GCHQ—Government Communications Headquarters

"In December 1902, Guglielmo Marconi made history by sending the first wireless radio message across the Atlantic. Remarkably, only two years later, Rudyard Kipling foretold the possibility of exploiting such radio messages to gather intelligence".[78]

---

[77] http://www.mathaba.net/data/sis/history.shtml
[78] CGHQ The uncensored story of Britain's most secret intelligence agency by Richard Aldrich published by Harper Collins 2011 pag 14

GCHQ was a branch of the Government Code and Cypher School (GC&CS), founded in November 1919. In the 1920s and 1930s, GC&CS proved successful in decipherin both German and Russian codes. When the German devised the Enigma machine in the 1930s, GC&CS intensified its endeavours. Right at the beginning of World War II in August 1939 the School relocated to Bletchley Park on the London suburbs. The first operation undertaken by cryptologists in the new headquarters was called Operation Ultra which consisted in the breaking of the Enigma ciphers, whose outlines were still classified in the 1970s. The School was the leading intelligence agency of the U.K. and in 1942 was renamed in order to protect its efforts: it was now the Government Communications Headquarters. In scope and activities GCHQ is very similar to the National Security Agency (NSA) of the United States. It also collaborates with NSA in the global oversight network called Echelon. A great deal of what the public knows about GCHQ is drawn from James Bamford's well-known book on NSA published in 1982.[79] Bamford opines that GCHQ had no less than 6 directorates at the time. These included:

- the Composite Signals Organization, which intercepted via-radio;
- the Directorate of Organization and Establishment, with administrative roles;
- the Directorate of Signals Intelligence Plans, which managed long-term plans;
- the Joint Technical Language Service, dedicated to the interception of foreign communications;
- the Directorate of Signals Intelligence Operations and Requirements, the biggest and most secretive, which Bamford thought to coordinate code-breaking operations;
- the Directorate of Communications Security, which cooperated with another agency, the Communications Electronics Security Group (CESG), founded in 1969, and serving as the British national technical authority for information security. The role

---

[79] "*The Puzzle Palace*" the first major, popular book devoted entirely to the history and workings of the National Security Agency.

of CESG is that of keep the communications safe through sophisticated equipment.

By the mid 1990s GCHQ counted 4,500 people employed. At the end of the Cold War, just few years before, the staff counted 6,000 people.

Structure GCHQ is led by the *Director of GCHQ*[80], and a Corporate Board, made up of Executive and Non-Executive Directors. *"Reporting to the Corporate Board is : Sigint missions (comprising Maths & cryptoanalysis, IT & computer systems, Linguists & translation and the Intelligence analysis unit), Enterprise (comprising Applied Research & emerging technologies, Corporate knowledge & information systems, Commercial supplier relationships and Biometrics),*

Corporate management (comprising Enterprise resource planning, Human resources, Internal audit and the Architecture team) and the Communications-Electronics Security Group"[81].

The GCHQ as we know it today is the result of a long structural evolution which began more than a century ago.

Signals Intelligence (Sigint) started its operations as a department composed of two small branches when World War I broke out and developed as a fully organized intelligence and security service in charge of the defence of the interests of the United Kingdom all over the world.

At the same time, ministerial and parliamentary surveillance measures have developed to make sure that GCHQ's actions and missions obey the law and that it does not operate out of proportions.

A constellation of acronyms has been used to name the Sigint and other Information Assurance institutions: Room 40, MI1b, GC&CS, LSIC, LCSA, CESD, CESG, among the others. The term GCHQ was first used, as we have said above, to uncover the Government Code and Cypher School when it moved in Bletchley Park in October 1939 and people living in that area began to inquire what was happening.

---

[80] http:/ /www.gsk.com/content/dam/gsk/globals/documents/pdf/eureka-science-witty-october-2010.pdf Iain Lobban at present. He became director in 2008

[81] Richard J. Aldrich, *GCHQ: The Uncensored Story of Britain's Most Secret Intelligence Agency*, London: Harper Collins, 2010, p. 565

Finally, GCHQ took its name officially on April 1, 1946. *GCHQ became an autonomous department on its own statutory footing, with ministerial responsibility belonging to the Secretary of State for Foreign and Commonwealth Affairs".*[82]

2.4.3 JIC-Joint Intelligence Committee

In 1936 the Committee of Imperial Defense, an agency which aim is to advise on the defence during peacetime, founded the Joint Intelligence Committee (JIC) as a branch of that committee, and during the War it was the major intelligence evaluation organization of the country. It relocated in 1957 to the Cabinet Office and its task was to prepare intelligence evaluation documents to pass to the committee.

The JIC is the main intelligence oversight organization of the U.K., it coordinates all the national intelligence agencies and advises the Cabinet for what security, foreign affairs and defence is concerned. It also controls and judge the priorities and targets of the three agencies of the U.K., SIS, Security Service and GCHQ, and provides the standards by which the intelligence work must be evaluated by the government.

In its turn, the JIC is also kept under surveillance by the Intelligence and Security Committee and is part of the Cabinet's Intelligence, Security and Resilience institution.

The JIC is led by a permanent member of the Senior Civil Service and assisted by an evaluation staff and the Intelligence and Security Secretariat. The staff is composed of experienced professional analysts taken from both the government an the army and complies with all the analyses on behalf of the committee. The reports made by the staff are compiled with information drawn from all the security and intelligence agencies of the country.

"Membership comprises the heads of the three collection agencies—the Secret Intelligence Service, Security Service and GCHQ—the Chief of Defense Intelligence, Deputy Chief of Defense Intelligence Staff, the Chief of the Assessment Staff, representatives of the Ministry of Defense, Foreign

---

[82] http://www.gchq.gov.uk/history/Pages/index.aspx History of GCHQ

and Commonwealth Office and other departments, and the Prime Minister's adviser on foreign affairs".[83]

The JIC has three functions:

- *"Advising the Prime Minister and Cabinet Ministers on intelligence collection and analysis priorities in support of national objectives.*
- *Directing the collection and analysis effort of the Secret Intelligence Service, Government Communications Headquarters, the Security Service and the Ministry of Defense based on those recommendations. The direction to the Ministry of Defense is implemented by Defense Intelligence.*
- *Assuring the professional standards of civilian intelligence analysis staff across the range of intelligence related activities in Her Majesty's Government"*[84].

Requirements and priorities

The JIC compiles the annual Requirements and Priorities which must be analyzed and approved by the Ministers. These priorities aim at supporting the security of the country:

- *"Protect UK and British territories, and British nationals and property, from a range of threats, including from terrorism and espionage;*
- *Protect and promote Britain's defense and foreign policy interests;*
- *Protect and promote the UK's economic well-being; and*
- *Support the prevention and detection of serious crime".*[85]

In recent years, the JIC was the centre of a controversy when it presented the notorious dossier about the Weapons of Mass Destruction in Iraq which led the U.K. government to declare war on the country. It

---

[83] http://www.princeton.edu/~achaney/tmve/wiki100k/docs/Joint_Intelligence_Committee_%28United_Kingdom%29.html "Joint Intelligence Committee (JIC), United Kingdom" (Princeton University)

[84] http://www.fas.org/irp/world/uk/jic/ "JIC Responsibilities"

[85] http://isc.independent.gov.uk/

was claimed that the document was purposely "blown up" before it was published in order to support the military intervention.

Dr. David Kelly, a government weapons expert who spoke his criticism on the dossier to journalists off-record, committed suicide after he found out that the government had been informed on his identity. The Hutton Inquiry sought to investigate on the case and evidence that the words and syntax of the dossier had been "strengthened" was brought to the Inquiry attention. But JIC member John Scarlett and head of MI6 Sir Richard Dearlove confirmed to the Inquiry that the wording of the dossier was compatible with their evaluation of the situation handed to the government. The US and UK Governments both announced investigations to clarify.

2.4.4 DI—Defense Intelligence

"Defense Intelligence can trace its roots back to 1946, when the Joint Intelligence Bureau (JIB) was established under the direction of General Kenneth Strong, General Eisenhower's wartime Chief of Intelligence"[86].

As a consequence of the unification of the Ministry of Defense in 1964, JIB and the other three intelligence agencies were mingled into a single organization called the Defense Intelligence Staff (DIS), and, as of 2009, it changed name into Defense Intelligence (DI).

Formerly dealing mainly with Cold War issues and Communism, now the DI is principally preoccupied in dealing with operations abroad, fighting the spreading of weapons of mass destruction and bolstering the war on terrorism, and the duties of the Chief of DI have now expanded in a series of tasks which go beyond the mere intelligence analysis to embrace also agents training and the gathering of geographical information.

The DI, now structural part of the Ministry of Defense, supplies the Armed Forces with strategic defense intelligence, as well as providing advice on the eventual employment and policy of the Armed Forces, supporting the research programs with the necessary equipment and guide military operations.

---

[86] https:/ /www.gov.uk/defence-intelligence "The History of DI"

DI also contributes both resources and personnel to the Joint Terrorism Analysis Centre (JTAC), which includes also members and resources from the other security and intelligence agencies of the U.K.

Not only the work of DI supports the U.K. government and helps to protect its interest, it also supports, through its assessments, the intelligence operations attended to by both the European Union and NATO.

The Chief of DI leads the coordination of intelligence operations also through the Armed Forces and reports to the Chief of the Defense Staff and the Permanent Secretary of the Ministry od Defense, assisted in this task by 2 deputies, 1 civilian and 1 military.

Meanwhile, the Deputy Chief of Defense Intelligence (DCDI) is in charge of the Defense Intelligence production, and the Assistant Chief of the Defense Staff collects, maps and trains intelligence staff. The Deputy also provides strategic warning on various topics, such as arms proliferation control and technical assessment of weapons systems.

GCHQ, SIS, The Security Service and Allied intelligence provide classified information for DI to assess. DI also draws upon other types of information, such as diplomatic records and a vast amount of media reports, including the internet.

ACDS(IC) collects all these disparate information in order to assist the defence and prepare a future intelligence strategy and policy for the government to use.

"To support its mission, Defense Intelligence has four essential roles:

- *Support to operations*
- *Support to contingency planning for operations*
- *Provision of early warning*
- *Provision of longer-term analysis of emerging threats".*
- *DI plays an integral part in the planning process throughout all stages of military operations, by providing intelligence collection and analysis at the tactical, operational and strategic levels.*
- *DI provides intelligence data and all source assessments that assist in preparations for future situations with the potential to require the commitment of UK Armed Forces. These products, which*

- *cover political and military developments, country and cultural information, critical infrastructure and internal security, all aid contingency planning.*
- *A fundamental responsibility of Defense Intelligence is to alert ministers, chiefs of staff, senior officials and defense planners to impending crises around the world. Such warning is vital for short—and medium-term planning.*
- *Defense Intelligence provides longer term assessments of likely scenarios around the world where UK Armed Forces might need to operate and of the equipment that they might face. It also provides technical support to the development of future military equipment and to the development of countermeasures against potentially hostile systems."*[87]

---

[87] https://www.gov.uk/defence-intelligence

CHAPTER THREE

THE CHIEFS OF MI6

3.1 Sir George Mansfield Smith-Cumming

Captain Sir George Mansfield Smith Cumming, a short, thick-set naval officer, was the founding father of the Secret Intelligence Service. Chief from 1909 to 1923. In October 1909 he took charge of the Foreign Section of the Secret Service Bureau that subsequently evolved into the independent service, SIS.

He was born on 1 April 1859 in British India, was the youngest son of Colonel John Thomas Smith of the Royal Engineers, of Föelallt House, Cardigan Kent, and his wife, Maria Sarah Tyser.

He married twice, firstly Dora Cloete in 1885 and after her death the extremely rich May Cumming and as part of the marriage settlement changed his surname from Smith to Smith-Cumming. Their only son, Alastair, a dangerous driver like his father, was killed in October 1914, driving Cumming's Rolls in France. According to an unconfirmed legend, Cumming himself hacked off his own broken leg with a penknife in the same accident and he has used his child's scooter to support his wooden leg.

According to his naval record he was *"a clever officer with great taste for electricity, who had a knowledge of photography, speaks French and draws well"*.[88]

Captain Cumming, or 'C' as he became known, the initial with which he marked in his customary green ink any documents he had

---

[88] Cit. A Century of Spies: Intelligence in the Twentieth Century by Jeffery T. Richelson pag 11

read. The famous author Ian Fleming took these aspects for his *"M"*, Sir Miles Messervy, using Cumming's other initial for the name and having *M* always write in green ink.

Cumming served on patrol in the East Indies, took part in operations against the Malay pirates, and was decorated for his role in the Egyptian campaign of 1882. However, Cumming not only had health problems but he increasingly suffered from severe seasickness, a rather unfortunate malady for a sailor, so *"in 1885 was placed on the retired list as "unfit for service"*.[89] Then he was assigned to an administrative role with the Royal Navy and in 1898, while still on the Royal Navy retired list, he was recruited by the foreign section of the Secret Service Bureau and established both the foreign section department and his own London flat at the top of 2 Whitehall Court.

"The early development of his organization was handicapped by its lack of founds and facilities, to the point that he complained he was unable to take a break away from his work because of the necessity of maintaining contact with his handful of sources, with whom he corresponded by the regular mail".[90]

Another big problem for C's organization was that it could not get good recruits because it was not supposed to exist.

Budgets were severely limited prior to World War I and Smith Cumming came to rely heavily on Sidney Reilley, a secret agent of dubious veracity based in Saint Petersburg. His early operations were directed almost entirely against Germany. Between 1909 and 1914 he recruited part-time casual agents in the shipping and arms business to keep track of naval construction in German shipyards and acquire other technical intelligence. He also had agents collecting German intelligence in Brussels, Rotterdam and St. Petersburg.

During the First World War, his most important network, "La Dame Blanche", had by January 1918 over 400 agents reporting on German troop movements from occupied Belgium and northern France. Cumming was less successful in post-revolutionary Russia. Despite a series of feats, his agents obtained little Russian intelligence of value.

---

[89] http://en.wikipedia.org/wiki/Mansfield_Smith-Cumming
[90] Cit At Her Majesty's Secret Service The Chiefs of Britain's Intelligence Agency MI6 by N. West pag 23

Secret Service budgets were once again severely cut after the end of WWI, and MI6 stations in Madrid, Lisbon, Zurich and Luxembourg were closed. Cumming succeeded, however, in gaining a monopoly of espionage and counter-intelligence outside Britain and the empire. He also established a network of SIS station commanders operating overseas under diplomatic cover.

Cumming died in 1923, just months before he was due to retire. His spirit lives on, however, not only in the use of his trademark green ink throughout the service, and the habit of referring to its chief as 'C', which endures today, but in the ethos with which he imbued the service he built.

3.2 Sir Hugh Sinclair

In 1923 the original *"C"*, Admiral Sir Mansfield Smith Cumming died and was replaced by the then Director of Naval Intelligence, *"Admiral Sir Quex Sinclair, so called because of the wickedest man in London in Sir Arthur Pinero's play "The Gay Lord Quex"*.[91] Hugh Sinclair, the son of Frederick Sinclair and his wife, Agnes May, was born in Southampton on 18th August 1873. He joined the Royal Navy at the age of thirteen in 1886. He was the head of MI6 from 1923 to 1939.

Sinclair was to prove an innovative Chief whose vision of the Agency ranged further afield than Cumming's, and in many aspects laid the foundations for the Cold War Agency.

During the 1919 Secret Service Committee deliberations the War Office' Director of Military Intelligence suggested that MI1(c) (so it was called in those days SIS) absorb the War Office's counter-intelligence organization MI5. Cumming rejected this opportunity on the grounds that, in his opinion there was no real connection between counter-espionage and the work of SIS. This was not a view shared by Sinclair who had a reputation as an anti-Bolshevik, sharing the 1919 Secret Service Committee's concerns about subversion operations conducted by Soviet agents in conjunction with domestic Communists.

---

[91] Cit At Her Majesty's Secret Service The Chiefs of Britain's Intelligence Agency MI6 by N. West pag 32

As a result, the new C began lobbying for SIS to absorb MI 5 and created his own Counter Espionage Section. Sinclair's concerns were not unfounded, indeed, a constant stream of Russian couriers bringing funds, propaganda and exhortation to Bolshevik sympathizers in Britain. A fourth liaison section was created in late 1929 with the establishment of the Royal Air Force as a Service department in its own right. The Air Section was to prove a source of considerable innovation within the Service, even undertaking the first systematic campaign of aerial photo-reconnaissance of Germany and the Mediterranean during the late 1930s." *In 1935 Sinclair set up a parallel, independent operational organization. This so called Z Organization"*[92] was to recruit its own agents, and run them completely independently of the Passport Control Office system operating on SIS funds. This was intended to serve as a fall-back in case the main SIS system was compromised. Despite the interwar additions of Section N, the CE Section and the Air Section, SIS' operational budget continued to decrease. Sinclair took the opportunity to expand the CE Section headquarters staff, and to set up CE stations in Holland and Belgium to cooperate with Dutch, Belgian and French security intelligence authorities against the Germans. He also made another innovation in SIS organization which would have far reaching consequences. In 1938 Section D was set up to investigate methods of sabotage and similar irregular warfare in peacetime and to implement them in wartime. Thus at the outbreak of war, the SIS consisted mainly in: Circulating Sections, Political, Military, Naval and Air; a small staff of G, officers overseeing and coordinating operations on a regional basis, the Passport Control Office on paper answerable directly to the Foreign Office but quartered at the SIS and staffed by it ; and three specialist operational sections, Section N, Section D and the CE Section. Of these sections, the Circulating Sections and Section N were the direct result of the demands of Whitehall consumers. For motives that remain so unfathomable, in late 1939 and before the actual outbreak of war, the Passport Control Office and Z Organizations were merged completely negating any benefits, the Z Organization might have afforded the Agency especially because the Hague station had been penetrated by

---

[92] A Short History of the British Secret Intelligence Service, MI-6 *Richard M. Bennett*

THE HISTORY OF MI6

the German secret services since 1935. As a result of its penetration, the Hague station was the target of a particularly elegant deception operation in which NAZI party Sicherheitdienst officers masqueraded as representatives of an anti-NAZI faction within Germany. This deception resulted in the kidnapping of both the PCO and the Z officer at "*Venlo*"[93] on the Dutch German border.

It has occasionally been suggested that the Venlo incident was a result of the SIS slipping the reigns of ministerial control, but according to the official history, documents available clearly indicated explicit Foreign Office, Prime Ministerial and eventually War Cabinet authorization of these clandestine negotiations.

On the fourth of November 1939, in the middle of the pre Venlo negotiations at the Hague station, Sinclair died, and after a round of dire Whitehall negotiations, his unofficial deputy and head of the Military Section, Stewart Menzies, was confirmed as the new C.

3.3 Major-General Sir Stewart Menzies

The man who assumed control at MI6/SIS from 1939 to 1952 was Stewart Menzies. The intelligence officer, was born in London, on 30 January 1890 and entered Eton College in 1903, where won prizes for languages.

"*Immediately on leaving school, in 1909, he was commissioned in the Grenadier Guards*"[94], but transferred to the Life Guards in the following year. While in the army he acquired a love of horses, reason why his

---

[93] http://ww2warstories.tripod.com/id7.htm A November 1939 counterespionage operation by the German Sicherheitsdienst (SD), under the command of Walter Schellenberg, the Venlo Incident enabled them to capture two British Secret Intelligence Service agents, at Venlo in the Netherlands, near the German border. Captured were Captain Sigismund Payne Best and Major Richard H. Stevens, who were held in German prisons throughout the war. A Dutch intelligence officer, Dirk Klops, was killed in the operation.

[94] Cit At Her Majesty's Secret Service The Chiefs of Britain's Intelligenge Agency MI6 by N. West pag 65

nickname *"Horse Guard"*.[95] Menzies first came into contact with the intelligence world during the First World War. The work appealed to him, and he showed a flair for it, aided by his knowledge of European languages. He ended the war with the rank of brevet major, and in 1919 was again selected for an intelligence appointment, this time with *"MI1(c)"*.[96]

Menzies was then known under the letter 'C' and took the lead of the SIS right after the war began. This was a very important moment for SIS and its history. After World War I and until the outbreak of the next war, the service suffered severly for a lack of both funds, equipments and resources: it was very ill organized for the challenging and global duties demanded by World War II. Between the wars, SIS had to deal with both enlargement and restoration, notwithstanding the complication to the overall situation brought in by the inconvenient hitch at Venlo. During these odd times the shape of SIS changed progressively but dramatically. Although the staff recruited by SIS was usually made of retired service officers, it now comprised talented everyday people and this posed a lot of management issues at the beginning. Moreover, Menzies had to deal with the complications introduced by the foundation of another secret service, the Special Operations Executive (SOE) as well as a new U.S. service who was trying to compete with SIS in neutral and enemy countries.

"These and other circumstances, as the lack of agents already in place in 1940 meant that it was to take some time before SIS could develop a momentum of its own and forge those links with allied intelligence and resistance organizations that were to prove valuable in the later stages of the war."[97] Sir Menzies was also the supervisor of the already mentioned Code and Cypher School (GCCS), which was responsible for the breaking of the German Enigma enciphering and deciphering machine[98], a device used thoroughly by all the German military system. By 1943,

---

95 "Horse Guards" was Sir Menzies' code name.
96 https:/ /www.sis.gov.uk/our-history/sis-or-mi6.html At that time the organization MI6 was formerly known as MI1(c).
97 http://www.oxforddnb.com/templates/article.jsp?articleid=34988&back=. Menzies, Sir Stuart Graham (Oxford Univeristy Press)
98 See § 1.8 and 2.4.2 of this book

GCCS was able to decode a large number of secret messages, to the great benefit of the allied forces.

The temper and toughness that Menzies displayed during the war years came as something of a surprise to those acquainted with his easy and affluent way of life between the wars. Running his service and supervising GCCS meant exceptionally long hours of office work, besides which he became in time a member of Churchill's intimate circle of war advisers. *"On such occasions he had to answer for more than his own responsibilities, for he was the only intelligence director to enjoy this privileged position. As an intelligence man his strength was a quickly understanding of operational issues and in his shrewd management of a network of powerful contacts.*

It was important his international influence and was a potent factor in establishing the Anglo-American and other allied intelligence alliances. During the war years his service had a greater role to play than ever before. By the time that he retired, in 1951, the pressures of the cold war had caused the intelligence world to develop in major ways and to acquire potent technological resources; it was a very different world from the one that Menzies had entered in 1919 but one in which, for SIS, the human source was still basic."[99]

3.4 Sir John Sinclair

"John Sinclair was the Chief of the service from 1953 to 1956. He was born in 1897. After being educated at Winchester and Dartmouth Naval College, he served as a midshipman in the Royal Navy for the first two years of the First World War"[100].

During that time he was almost continuously at sea, mainly in submarines, but scarcely ever free from seasickness. He had to be invalided out of the navy after only six years' service. His convalescence was long but Sinclair was able to return to West Downs School to do

---

[99] http://www.oxforddnb.com/templates/article.jsp?articleid=34988&back=. (quoted)

[100] Cit At Her Majesty's Secret Service The Chiefs of Britain's Intelligenge Agency MI6 by N. West pag 64

some teaching until well enough to apply for a new career in the army. In 1918 he entered the Royal Military Academy. Commissioned in the Royal Field Artillery in 1919, he served first with the Murmansk force in northern Russia and then in India. He returned to duty at Aldershot, and married in 1927 Esme Beatrice.

A successful officer Sinclair became Deputy Director of Military operations during the Second World War.

Intelligence played a great part in the war and was at that time needed more than ever. He quickly showed that he had the qualities for the job; a capacity for detail, good judgment and a ready acceptance of responsibility. Sinbad Sinclair, as he was called by his colleagues, became a much respected DMI and held the post until the end of the war.

Near the expected end of his military career a new prospect opened for Sinclair.

Sinclair succeeded Sir Menzies in 1953, when he became the MI6 Director General. The director of MI6, the civilian intelligence service responsible to the foreign secretary and the prime minister. The choice of a successful DMI, admired for his strong character and organizational skills, was particularly appropriate for the transitional period that lay ahead of the service. A large wartime organization had to be scaled down, new methods and standards of recruitment for permanent staff agreed, and old international alliances renegotiated for new peacetime tasks. He achieved these things in ways that lasted well, while at the same time directing current operations in his usual practical and responsible way. It was therefore unfair to his reputation that the only time he came to public notice was in connection with the intelligence operation of 19 April 1956 in which the diver *"Commander Lionel Crabb"*,[101] disappeared in April 1956 on a secret mission to investigate the Russian cruiser Ordkhonikidze. This created a diplomatic row as the ship had brought over Nikita Khrushchev and Nikolai Bulganin on a goodwill mission to Britain. Sir Anthony Eden (The British Prime Minister) was furious and as a result forced Sinclair to resign. He was replaced by Sir Dick White, the former head of MI6. Sir John Sinclair died in 1977.

---

[101] http:/ /www.bbc.co.uk/insideout/south/series11/index_mobile_phones_bugging.shtml
"an underwater sabotage expert" who disappeared in a secret mission.

3.5 Sir Dick White

Sir Dick White was the chief of SIS from 1956 to 1968.

He was born on 20 December 1906 in Kent. White's early childhood was comfortable, but his father was over ambitious in business and careless with money, and in 1913 the family endured a financial crash. White never forgot the shock of the sudden collapse into near penury. In 1917 he was sent to Bishop's Stortford College.

"His career began in 1934 when he met, in a British public school tour of Australia and New Zealand, Lieutenant Colonel Malcolm Cumming, who subsequently joined the security service"[102]. Cumming had been impressed by White, and duly recommended him to his MI5 superiors for appointment.

White was the first recruit to join the Security Service as a graduate and became its director general from 1953 to 1956. During that years, he enjoyed some success against individual German intelligence operations. Within MI5 White, along with other officers played a crucial role in the subtle development of double cross.

After three years at the helm in MI5 White was abruptly transplanted to the very different world of SIS. This unexpected move was a consequence of the Commander Crabbe incident, a freelance SIS operation which went disastrously and publicly wrong. The head of SIS, Sir John Sinclair, was pushed out, and White was offered his post. He accepted out of duty, not ambition: he liked running MI5. He had no personal experience of foreign intelligence gathering he once ruefully remarked to a subordinate that he wished that he had run agents in the field, as he felt that he would then have had a better grasp of the human pressures under which SIS officers worked but he had vast knowledge of counter-intelligence, he understood Whitehall, he had excellent international contacts, and he could manage.

As head of SIS his approach, once he had imposed a necessary reorganization, was to concentrate on the service's external relations with Whitehall and the wider world and to let his directors get on with their jobs, a style which contributed to a perception among some field officers that he was aloof and out of touch.

---

[102] http:/ /www.independent.co.uk/news/people/obituary-sir-dick-white

White's achievements as head of SIS are hard to estimate. He undoubtedly succeeded in restoring morale and in improving relations with the Foreign Office and the Cabinet Office. But secret intelligence operations of their nature are not intended to become public knowledge for a very long time, if ever, and it is uncertain what the organization did or failed to do under White's direction in cold war and other spheres of activity. His presence as head of SIS, went far towards repairing Britain's standing with the American intelligence community.

When the time came for White to retire in 1968, the selection of a successor proved difficult. On his retirement from SIS, White was appointed to the newly created post of coordinator of intelligence in the Cabinet Office. The appointment of White to this novel position was not without its critics. White avoided any temptation to turn the post into an over lordship of the various intelligence agencies or otherwise to throw his weight around, and instead concentrated on giving advice when asked. Some argue that this approach was tantamount to doing nothing at all, but there is no doubt that White's personal contribution was valued in the Cabinet Office. *"In 1972, feeling rather worn out, he retired from Whitehall for good and died after a long illness on 21 February 1993".*[103]

3.6 SIR Rennie, John Ogilvy

He was the 6th 'C' of the Secret Intelligence Service from 1968 to 1973. *"A diplomatist and intelligence officer, was born on 13 January 1914 in London. He was educated at Wellington College and Balliol College, Oxford, where he showed precocious talent as a painter".*[104] On leaving Oxford in 1935, Sir John Rennie joined the advertising agency in New York. In 1938 he married a Swiss subject, Anne-Marie Céline Monica.

After the outbreak of the Second World War, Rennie joined the staff of the British consulate in Baltimore, combating German propaganda.

---

[103] Cit At Her Majesty's Secret Service The Chiefs of Britain's Intelligence Agency MI6 by N. West pag 125

[104] http:/ /www.telegraph.co.uk/news/uknews/law-and-order/Career--the -chief-of-MI6.html

THE HISTORY OF MI6

From 1942 to 1946 he worked in New York as head of the section producing radio programs designed to put across the British viewpoint.

In January 1946 he was formally accepted into the foreign service and on his return to London in December that year was appropriately posted to the Foreign Office's information policy department.

In March 1949 Rennie was appointed first secretary in Washington, where he began to establish his reputation in the foreign service, and he was transferred to Warsaw with similar duties in June 1951.

Amid continuing suspicion within the Labour government over some of the activities of the Secret Intelligence Service, or MI6, Rennie was appointed in spring 1968 to replace Sir Dick White as 'C', the head of the service. The deliberate choice of an outsider angered many within the service and made life very difficult for Rennie.

For three months Maurice Oldfield, who had been White's deputy and as such, under SIS tradition, his anointed successor, ran the service on his own, ensuring that all important operational information came direct to him and not to Rennie. In Oldfield's opinion, Rennie was *"disastrously slow to act, always looking over his shoulder and far too apt to seek unworkable compromises"*. [105]Although the two men eventually achieved a *modus vivendi*, their relationship was never easy. Oldfield continued to oppose many of Rennie's decisions, including on the grounds that the SIS traditionally operated only in foreign territory, his agreement to the request in 1971 of the Conservative prime minister Edward Heath that SIS send an officer to Northern Ireland with a brief to make contact with the "street communities". It was the initial contacts between this SIS officer, Frank Steele, and two young republicans, Gerry Adams and Martin McGuinness, that led to the so-called "back-channel" and eventually to the Northern Ireland peace process.

Rennie suffered further family tragedy when his son Charles and his daughter-in-law were sent to geol on drugs charges in 1973. This incident was widely publicized after the story, involving Rennie's identity. His offer to resign was turned down and he continued in charge of SIS until his official retirement date in January 1974, when he was succeeded by Oldfield. He died on 30 September 1981 at St Thomas's Hospital, Lambeth.

---

[105] *www.oxforddnb.com/ltemplates/article*

3.7 Sir Oldfield, Sir Maurice

"Maurice Oldfield was Chief of the Secret Intelligence Service from 1973 to 1978".[106] He was born on 16 November 1915 in Derbyshire. In 1934 he won a scholarship to Manchester University and specialized in medieval history. After the award of the Thomas Brown memorial prize, in 1938 he graduated with first class honors in history and was elected to a fellowship. The war upset his plans for an Sir academic career.

After joining the intelligence corps, Oldfield's service was spent mostly at the Cairo headquarters of security intelligence Middle East.

Following a short spell in London from 1958 to 1959, Oldfield was selected for the key post of SIS representative in Washington, where he remained for the next four years, with the main task of cultivating good relations with the Central Intelligence Agency (CIA). His close ties with James Angleton, the head of the CIA's counter-intelligence branch, were reinforced by their shared interest in medieval history. But Angleton also persuaded Oldfield to swallow the outpourings of the KGB defector, Anatoly Golitsyn, who was claiming, also that the Sino-Soviet conflict and President Tito of Yugoslavia's breach with Moscow were clear cases of Soviet disinformation. Soon after leaving Washington, Oldfield didn't confess his errors with overt explanation.

On his return to London, Oldfield became director of counter-intelligence and in 1965 C's deputy. He therefore had reason to feel aggrieved when he was passed over in 1968 in favour of Sir John Rennie from the Foreign and Commonwealth Office, whom he later succeeded as C in 1973. This made Oldfield the first member of the post-war intake to reach the top post. Under his leadership, SIS benefited from the good relations he cultivated with both Conservative and Labour ministers at home and from its improved standing with friendly foreign intelligence services with which he kept in personal touch. *"Oldfield was appointed KCMG in 1975 and GCMG on his retirement in 1978: the only C so far to have received this award"*.[107] He was also the first to cultivate chosen journalists at meetings in the Athenaeum. In 1978, he began

---

[106] Cit At Her Majesty's Secret Service The Chiefs of Britain's Intelligence Agency MI6 by N. West pag 142
[107] http://www.oxforddnb.com/view/theme

a study of Captain Sir Mansfield Cumming, the first C, but soon lost interest in it through lack of material. He therefore welcomed Margaret Thatcher's proposal in October 1979 to appoint him coordinator of security intelligence in Northern Ireland. In Belfast he did his best to improve relations between the chief constable and the new general officer commanding, but the strains of office soon told on him. It was not only incipient cancer, but also alleged evidence on his unprofessional contacts that caused his return to London in June 1980. Subsequent interrogation resulted in the withdrawal of his positive vetting certificate, after he confessed he had lied to cover up his homosexuality. There is, however, no evidence that his private life had prejudiced the security of his work at any stage in his career. He died, in London on 11 March 1981. *"Six years after his death in 1981 the prime minister, Margaret Thatcher, confirmed that he had been an active homosexual"*.[108]

3.8 Franks, Sir Arthur Temple

"Sir Arthur Temple (Franks) was born on 13 July 1920 in London. In 1934 his parents sent him to Rugby School and in 1938 he went to Queen's College, Oxford, obtaining a war-shortened law degree in 1940, before joining the Royal Corps of Signals in August that year"[109].

Short-sighted but absolutely fit, Franks was commissioned into the Hertfordshire regiment in September 1941 and posted to the Middle East during 1942 as a battalion intelligence officer to the Libyan Arab force in the western desert. In July 1943, two months after the final defeat of axis forces in north Africa, he was promoted to staff captain and in September joined the Special Operations Executive (SOE), Britain's wartime clandestine sabotage agency participating in numerous operations.

Franks was demobilized in June 1946, at first undertaking provincial press work for Staffordshire Sentinel Newspapers Ltd, and then joining

---

[108] http://www.telegraph.co.uk/news/obituaries/1554671/Betty-Kemp.html
[109] http://www.independent.co.uk/news/obituaries/sir-dick-franks-wartime-soe-officer-who-became-chief-of-the-secret-intelligence-service-in-the-cold-war

the *Daily Mirror* in May 1948 as a sub-editor. Only a year after joining the *Daily Mirror* he was recruited into the Secret Intelligence Service (SIS), or MI6 as it was popularly known. The qualities he had shown while working for SOE must have been attractive to SIS, an organization now fully engaged in the emerging cold war.

Franks's first overseas posting was to Cyprus in October 1952, where he covered Middle Eastern affairs. Despite his youth and relative inexperience he served in Tehran from 1953 to 1956, carrying out well the very difficult job of maintaining contact with the new young shah of Iran, who had just been restored to the throne. His wife, Rachel, was active socially while in Tehran and the couple proved popular then as subsequently within the diplomatic corps. His next major posting abroad was to Bonn in July 1962, where he stayed for four years and struck up a lifelong friendship with David Cornwell, the spy novelist known as John Le Carré. His posting to Bonn, a key station in SIS's targeting of Soviet bloc countries, indicated that senior management within SIS had come to regard him as one of the service's most outstanding officers among his peer group. During the 1970s his reputation continued to rise within SIS and he eventually became assistant chief of SIS in 1977. Throughout this period he showed himself to be an all-round performer, who could produce far-seeing plans coupled to realistic recommendations for practical action. One of his best attributes was his ability to identify the important while firmly rejecting the trivial.

It came as no surprise when Franks succeeded Sir Maurice Oldfield as chief of SIS in February 1978, a post he held until 1981. Reportedly he told his board of directors at his first staff meeting as chief that 'I want the Directors' Board to be a collegiate body." *I will be listening to you, you will not be listening to me*".[110] As chief he sought to get the best out of his staff and to continue to develop good relations with Whitehall and, in particular, the Foreign and Commonwealth Office. Indeed he was regarded not only as a first-rate political operator but also as an able organizer with a sure touch for staff management and the gift of generating loyalty; it was these attributes that helped to continue to professionalize the service and kept morale high under his leadership. After his career in SIS had finished Franks accepted a job

---

[110] http://www.guardian.co.uk/uk/2008/oct/28/sir-arthur-franks-obituary

with the Wilkinson Group, advising on their overseas marketing of civil protection products. In retirement he purposely kept a low profile, refusing to talk about his career in SIS by making himself inaccessible to researchers and journalists. Throughout his life he always found time for his family, to whom he was devoted, and for the Travellers' Club, which he greatly enjoyed. He died of cancer of the liver at Aldeburgh Hospital, Park Road, Aldeburgh, on 12 October 2008.

3.9 Figures, Sir Colin Frederick

"He directed the organization SIS from 1981 to1985".[111] Intelligence officer, was born on 1 July 1925. He was educated at King Edward's School, Birmingham and joined the Secret Intelligence Service (Mi6) directly from university in 1951. His reputation within the service for competence and reliability was by this time growing into the realization that he was potentially a high-flying senior officer. In 1956 he had married a secretary at the Foreign Office, Pamela Ann Timmis, with whom he had a son and two daughters. He broadened his relationship with the Foreign and Commonwealth Office and, especially during four years directing SIS operations in Northern Ireland, with the Security Service and the military.

Figures was a natural choice to take over as deputy chief of SIS under Sir Arthur (Dickie) Franks in 1979, then to replace him as chief in 1981. Figures's four years as chief were conspicuously successful. He combined a background founded on solid midland middle-class values with practical common sense and an ability to lead by example. *"Self-effacing but quietly self-confident in manner, he exemplified SIS's stated policy of employing not risk seekers but risk takers"*.[112] He was approachable by the whole staff, a good delegator who was liked, respected, and trusted by his subordinates. A man of total integrity, he combined an infectious sense of humor with an absence of pomposity; never a puritan, he was always staunchly loyal to his family and he was unusually fortunate in having

---

[111] Cit At Her Majesty's Secret Service The Chiefs of Britain's Intelligenge Agency MI6 by N. West pag 187
[112] http://www.guardian.co.uk/uk/2008/oct/28/sir-arthur-franks-obituary

a wife who also established herself firmly in the affections of the service and took great interest in questions of welfare in what could sometimes be quite stressful professional circumstances.

"*Figures had not been long in the chair when Argentina invaded the Falkland Islands in 1982*"[113]. SIS initially came in for some criticism for not having forecast the invasion, as did the Foreign and Commonwealth Office, but it was soon rightly accepted that foreign intelligence and diplomatic services faced an impossible task in monitoring the unpredictable policies of an erratic dictator. More importantly, and with some invaluable help from their excellent relationships with allied liaison services in North and South America, western Europe, and the Commonwealth, SIS was able to contribute significantly to the achievements of the armed forces in their successful military campaign. Among SIS's achievements was the monitoring of the commercial availability of *exocet* missiles that might have replenished Argentinian stocks, the missiles having been deployed with considerable effect against the Royal Navy at a time when the outcome of the campaign was still far from clear. SIS was also able to complement Government Communications Headquarters (GCHQ) in reporting on the Argentinian air force and navy. A less glamorous preoccupation for Figures as chief of SIS was the growing Treasury pressure to trim the budgets of the intelligence community and to improve the working relationships between SIS, the Security Service, and GCHQ. Rigorous financial controls were imposed by the Treasury, but making good use of his high reputation and popularity in the intelligence community Figures presided over four harmonious and successful years for British intelligence. One of his outstanding achievements in this period was the reorganization of the intelligence machinery in Northern Ireland, especially after the Ballygawley incident of August 1988, when eight British soldiers were killed and twenty-eight injured by an IRA bomb. His previous responsibility for SIS operations in the territory gave him an invaluable background for this task and meant that his views carried appropriate weight.

---

[113] http: / /www.telegraph.co.uk/news/obituaries/1537476/Sir-Colin-Figures.html

After his retirement in 1989 Figures and his wife divided their time between Thames Ditton, Surrey, and the Isle of Wight. During the last few years of his life he became increasingly incapacitated by Parkinson's disease. On 8 December 2006 he died.

3.10 Sir Christopher Keith Curwen

Sir Christopher Keith Curwen, the son of a vicar, was born on 9 April, 1929." *He succeeded Sir Colin Figures as Head of the British Secret Intelligence Service from 1985 to 1989.*
Educated at Sherborne School and Sidney Sussex College, Cambridge, he was commissioned into the 4th Queen's Own Hussars in 1948". [114]*Then he joined the Secret Intelligence Service and became a South-East Asia specialist before being posted to Geneva and Washington D.C.*

Despite his personal setback, Curwen's appointment had been uncontroversial and he had the advantage of burgeoning budget. The Prime Minister, now fully convinced of the value of Intelligence, after years of financial cuts, allowed SIS to expand and to find the money to fund the increase.

Curwen remained at his post for just four years, during his service the main operations were addressed towards Soviet espionage.

A double *"Oleg Gordievsky"*, [115]seems to have begun to symphatise with Western beliefs and began his active collaboration with British, and later American, intelligence agencies.

"Two of Gordievsky's most important contributions were averting a potential nuclear confrontation with the Soviet Union when NATO exercise Able Archer 83 was mis-interpreted by the Soviets as a potential first strike, and identifying Mikhail Gorbachev as the Soviet heir apparent long before he came to prominence."[116]

---

[114] Cit At Her Majesty's Secret Service The Chiefs of Britain's Intelligence Agency MI6 by N. West pag 204
[115] http ://www.nationalcoldwarexhibition.org/explore/biography.Gordievsky
[116] http://news.bbc.co.uk/2/hi/europe/8184338.stm. (Gordon Corera, 'How vital were Cold War spies?', BBC News, 5 August 2009)

Sir Christopher Keith Curwen retired in 1989 and was replaced by Sir Colin Hugh Verel McColl.

3.11 Sir Colin Hugh Verel McColl

"Sir Colin Hugh Verel McColl was born on 6 September 1932 was the head of the British Secret Intelligence Service from 1989 to 1994".[117]

Educated at Sharewsbury School and at the Queen's College Oxford. McColl, joined Her Majesty's Diplomatic Service in 1950 and spent his first two postings in Laos and Vietnam. He spent the mid-'60s in Warsaw, where he forged a reputation as a far-sighted and competent officer, and his last overseas posting was to Geneva in 1973 as head of station.

In April 1989 Sir Colin was appointed Chief of MI-6 where he served until he retired in 1994. Prime Minister John Major unexpectedly acknowledged that Sir Colin was the head of the British Secret Intelligence Service.

Mr. Major's revelation before the House of Commons was surprising, but it was not news. Sir Colin's title was one of Britain's most open secrets. Until now, however, no one in the Government ever officially acknowledged what Sir Colin did.

"Speaking on the first day of the new Parliament session, Mr. Major said he was coming clean with one of Britain's most public secrets to emphasize his commitment to press forward government reforms and sweep away some of secrecy which needlessly covered too much of government business".[118]

Sir Colin Hugh Verel McColl was Counsellor in the Foreign and Commonwealth Office since 1977. But what was widely known, unofficially, was that he was named to head the Secret Intelligence

---

[117] Cit At Her Majesty's Secret Service The Chiefs of Britain's Intelligence Agency MI6 by N. West pag 214

[118] http://www.nytimes.com/1992/05/07/world/the-secret-s-out-top-british-spy-identified.html

THE HISTORY OF MI6

Service in 1989 by Prime Minister Margaret Thatcher. A year later, he received his *"knighthood"*[119].

In retirement he was a Director of the Scottish American Investment Company.

In 1995 Sir Colin became an advisory director of the independent private equity advisory firm, Campbell Lutyens. He has also served on the advisory board of the Dr Magnus Ranstorp Centre for the Study of Terrorism and Political Violence at St Andrews University, and currently serves on the International Advisory Board of Oxford Analytica.

Founded in 1975, Oxford Analytica is a consulting firm that provides strategic political, economic and social analysis on the implications of world developments. They do this through tailored consultancy studies and, each week day, through the Oxford Analytica Daily Brief.

Sir Colin capped a distinguished career of government service by heading the UK's MI-6 for several years. Now retired, he has been working on ways in which decision makers in both the public and private sectors might most usefully think about and quantify risk.

3.12 Sir David Spedding

David Spedding was the Secret Intelligence Service's 11th Chief since its foundation in 1909.

He was born on 7 March 1943, the son of an Army colonel. He went to Sherborne and from there to Hertford College, Oxford, from which he graduated in Mediaeval History. [120]It was in 1967, during his time as a post-graduate student at Oxford, aged 24, that he was recruited into MI6 taking part in several missions. He generally described as devious, callous and calculating but was also the man who brought MI6 fully into the post-Cold War world, setting up the Global Issues Controllerate to

---

[119] http:/ /www.royal.gov.uk/MonarchUK/Honours/Knighthoods.aspx A knighthood or a dame hood, its female equivalent is one of the highest honours an individual in the United Kingdom can achieve.

[120] Cit At Her Majesty's Secret Service The Chiefs of Britain's Intelligence Agency MI6 by N. West pag 229

address the threats of crime and weapons proliferation. Anti-narcotics policing was to become one of the service's most successful roles.

Professionally, he made his name in the successful running of a section set up to counter Middle Eastern terrorism, then underlined it by his outstanding performance as SIS's controller for the Middle East during the Gulf War. He was a good speaker, clear-thinking, resonant and unforced, and his lectures were popular for years after. As "C", he won wide respect in Whitehall, where he was acknowledged not only as a safe pair of hands—an essential quality in any "C" but as a tenacious fighter of his service's corner.

Whether as a junior case officer, recruiting and running agents, or as a Whitehall mandarin on Cabinet Office committees, his dedication, methodical procedure, attention to detail, formidable memory, obvious good nature and natural fair-mindedness won him respect and affection. Like nearly all successful people, he was very hard-working; but unlike many, he always appeared to have time.

But if Spedding's reorganization of the service to make its work more appropriate to the post-Cold War world was highly successful, his time as "C", the traditional title for the head of MI6, was dogged by controversy.

He was amongst those who helped to organize the service's move from Century House to the ostentatious £236 million new building on the south bank of the Thames at Vauxhall Cross,[121] *criticized by some for giving the service too high a public profile.*

"Spedding's appointment as head of MI6 in September 1994 came at a time when the service was under intense scrutiny, which had been prompted by Sir Richard Scott's Inquiry into the Matrix Churchill affair. MI6 had used Paul Henderson, the British managing director of the Iraqi-owned Matrix Churchill, to collect information on Iraq's attempts to build a supergun which would allow it to threaten Israel.

His period in charge also saw the unfolding of the Tomlinson affair, in which Richard Tomlinson, a junior officer sacked a year into Spedding's

---

[121] http://www.telegraph.co.uk/news/obituaries/1309010/Sir-David-Spedding.html

tenure, took his grievances to the newspapers, sparking a series of stories critical of MI6".[122] He died aged 58.

3.13 Sir Richard Dearlove

"He became the second MI6 chief to be named publicly, when he was appointed head of the secret intelligence service in 1999".[123]

Described as an intelligence "all-rounder", his appointment was seen as a reflection of the agency's new post-Cold War priorities, fighting organized crime rather than spying on the Soviets. Chosen by then Foreign Secretary, Robin Cook, in consultation with the Prime Minister, Tony Blair, Sir Richard took the classic route into the espionage business. *"Born in Cornwall on 23 January 1945, he was educated at the independent fee-paying Monkton Combe School near Bath".*[124]

After a year at Kent School in the United States, he went to Queen's College, Cambridge, a favorite recruiting ground for the intelligence agencies, where he was almost certainly "talent spotted". He began his MI6 career at the age of 21 after graduating in 1966 and two years later received his first overseas posting to the Kenyan capital, Nairobi.

After postings in Prague, Paris and Geneva, Sir Richard became head of MI6's Washington station in 1991.

He returned to the UK in 1993 as director of personnel and administration and became director of operations the following year.

In 1999 Sir Richard was appointed chief and, like all his predecessors since the agency's founder Captain Sir Mansfield Cumming, became known in Whitehall simply as "C".

A year later he had to endure the indignity of a terrorist rocket attack—blamed on dissident Irish republicans—on MI6's headquarters on the south bank of the River Thames, although the damage was slight.

---

[122] http://www.telegraph.co.uk/news/obituaries/1309010/Sir-David-Spedding.html

[123] http:/ /www.telegraph.co.uk/news/celebritynews/1925383/MI6-chief-Sir-Richard-Dearlove

[124] http:/ /www.telegraph.co.uk/education/universityeducation/8860407/Security-blunder-at-MI6

Sir Richard, who is married with three grown-up children, received a knighthood in June 2001. Later that year, the agency's reputation came under fire after the 11 September attacks on the World Trade Centre and the Pentagon.

MI6 was accused by the Parliamentary Intelligence and Security Committee of failing to respond with sufficient urgency to warnings that al-Qaeda was planning a major terrorist attack.

The agency came in for more scrutiny after the government's decision to publish an Iraqi weapons dossier based on secret intelligence.

But reports of a rift between the government and Sir Richard over the issue, were denied by ministers.

The Foreign Office stressed Sir Richard's retirement in August 2004—after the normal five year length of service for a head of MI6—was in no way connected to events relating to Iraq.

Sir Richard raised the issue again in a 2007 lecture on intelligence and the media.

He said the government felt using intelligence as the primary justification for its actions was the best chance of winning over its opponents but it turned out to have highly undesirable consequences for the intelligence community.

Sir Richard took up the position of Master of Cambridge University's Pembroke College after leaving MI6.

"In February 2008, he was called to appear at the inquest into the death of Princess Diana and Dodi Al Fayed."[125] He denied claims by Harrods boss Mohammed Al Fayed that the intelligence services killed the princess and his son, who died in a car crash in Paris in August 1997.

Dearlove retired from MI6 in August 2005.

3.14 Sir John McLeod Scarlett

"Sir John was born in 1948 in London and educated at Magdalen College, Oxford"[126], where, in 1970, he was awarded First Class Honours

---

[125] http:/ /news.bbc.co.uk/2/hi/uk_news/7026611.stm

[126] Cit http:/ /www.dailymail.co.uk/news/article-2210692/Sir-John-Scarlett-Former-MI6-chief

THE HISTORY OF MI6

in Modern History. Sir John Scarlett served as Chief of the British Secret Intelligence Service from 2004 to 2009. Sir John joined the SIS in 1971 and over the next 20 years served in Nairobi, Paris and twice in Moscow as well as several assignments in London covering the Middle East, Africa, Eastern Europe and the Soviet Union. His second time in Moscow (1991-1994) coincided with the end of the USSR and the early years of the Russian Federation. In early September 2001, he retired from SIS on appointment as Chairman of the Joint Intelligence Committee (JIC) in the Cabinet Office.

Sir John took up the appointment at the JIC one week before the September 11 attacks. During the following three years, he was responsible for the co-ordination and presentation of intelligence advice to the Prime Minister and senior members of the Government. On the 1st of August 2004, Sir John rejoined SIS as its Chief until 2009.

As Head of the Service, he was responsible for the management of resources, the conduct of operations, and advice to the Government during a period of significant global uncertainty and risk from international terrorism, regional instability and potential conflict; and major shifts in the global balance of power. *"Sir John was appointed OBE (Officer of the British Empire) in 1987, CMG (Commander of St Michael and St George) in 2001 and KCMG in 2007".*[127] In 2011 Sir John was appointed Officer of the Légion d'Honneur. He was severely criticized in the media by some who believe that certain honors have been given unfairly to officials and supporters loyal to the government during the 2003 war in Iraq. Scarlett, while Chairman of the JIC, was the principal author of the assessments on which the *"September Dossier"*[128] was based, a document partly by which the Prime Minister justified to Parliament

---

[127] http://www.telegraph.co.uk/finance/newsbysector/industry/defence/9576799/Former-head-of-MI6

[128] http: //en.wikipedia.org/wiki/September_Dossier A 2003 briefing document for the Blair Labour government. It was issued to journalists on 3 February 2003 by Alastair Campbell, Blair's Director of Communications and Strategy, and concerned Iraq and weapons of mass destruction. Together with the earlier September Dossier, these documents were ultimately used by the government to justify its involvement in the invasion of Iraq.

the invasion of Iraq and which was later found to be flawed. However, despite the claims of preferential honors, the award of a KCMG is normal practice for all heads of SIS and senior FCO and British diplomats.

Sir John retired on 31st October 2009 after 38 years in Government Service.

3.15 Sir John Sawers

Sir John Sawers, was born 26 July 1955. Born in Warnick. *"Sawers was brought up in a family of five children In Bath and educated at the City of Bath Boys' School, where he still holds the 440 yard hurdles school record"*[129].

He and his wife Shelly have three children.

He is a British diplomat and senior civil servant, moreover the current Chief of the Secret Intelligence Service (MI6). Sir John sawers was previously the British Permanent Representative to the United Nations from August 2007 to November 2009.

It is highly unusual for a diplomat, or any outsider, to be appointed as the head or C for chief of Britain's secret intelligence service.

Sawers joined the Foreign and Commonwealth Office in 1977.

In his early career, Sawers worked in Yemen and Syria, which according to some reports was on behalf of MI6. He became Political Officer in Damascus in 1982 and then returned to the Foreign & Commonwealth Office to take up the roles of Desk Officer in the European Union European Department in 1984 and Private Secretary to the Minister of State in 1986. He was based in Pretoria and then Cape Town in South Africa from 1988 to 1991 during the first part of the transition from apartheid. He returned to the Foreign & Commonwealth Office yet again to take up the roles of Head of European Union Presidency Planning Unit in 1991 and Principal Private Secretary to Douglas Hurd in 1993. The period was dominated by war in Bosni, crises in the Middle East, and the debate in Britain on the European Union. From 1995 to 1998 he was in the United States and spent a year

---

[129] http://www.guardian.co.uk/politics/2009/jun/16/sir-john-sawers-mi6-chief

as an International Fellow at Harvard University and later working at the British Embassy in Washington D.C., where he headed the Foreign and Defense Policy team. From January 1999 to summer 2001 he was Foreign Affairs Adviser to Prime Minister Tony, dealing with all aspects of Foreign and Defense Policy and working closely with international counterparts. The period included the Kosovo War. He also worked on the Northern Ireland peace process and the implementation of the Good Friday Agreement.

He reviewed the Iraq sanctions policy during this period and issued a document that included consideration of regime change. He served two years in the Middle east as Ambassador to Egypt from 2001 to 2003, and for three months was the British Government's Special Representative in Baghdad assisting in the establishment of the Coalition Provisional Authority as the transitional government during the occupation in Iraq occupation in Iraq. In August 2003 Sawers was appointed Director General for Political Affairs at the Foreign and Commonwealth Office. In this post he advised the Foreign Secretary on political and security issues worldwide and negotiated on behalf of the Foreign Secretary with international partners in the G8, EU and the UN. He was particularly closely involved in policy on Iran, Iraq, Afghanistan and the Balkans. Sawers headed the British team in the EU-3 negotiations over Iran's nuclear program in 2006, utilizing his scientific background on nuclear matters. "*Sawers was announced as the new chief of the Secret Intelligence on 16 June 2009, succeeding Sir John Scarlett. He took up his new appointment in November 2009, soon after MI6 celebrates its 100th anniversary*".[130]

Like his predecessors, the head of MI6 still signs letters and memos "C", written in green ink following the tradition of the spy agency's eccentric founder.

---

[130] http:/ /www.telegraph.co.uk/news/uknews/law-and-order/5551402/Career-civil-servant-the-new-chief-of-MI6.html

Chapter Four

SIS SPECIAL OPERATIONS

As we know MI6 is one of the most secretive British agency, till date not much is known about its overall budget and also about the number of members who are currently serving the prestigious organization. However, something is known about some of MI6's most famous missions.

4.1 Cupcake operation

In June 2011, some newspapers reported news of what is now Known as *"cupcake operation"*. Though humorous to hear, it was one of the most challenging mission.

British spies have ruined *Al Qaeda's plans to recruit terrorists*[131] by a new English-language magazine by replaced bomb-making instructions on the website with recipes for cupcakes.

The terror group's online magazine *"Inspire"* had contained a 67 page guide for its *followers on how to "Make a bomb in the Kitchen of Your Mom" by "The AQ Chef"*.[132]

However, after intelligence agency MI6, partnering with the U.K. Government Communications Headquarters, or GCHQ, also part of a Her Majesty's Government's Signal Intelligence hacked into "Inspire,"

---

[131] Al Qaeda attempted to recruit a new generation of so-called 'lone wolf' terrorists. 124 http://www.telegraph.co.uk/news/uknews/terrorism-in-the-uk/8553366/MI6-attacks-al-Qaeda-in- Operation-Cupcake.html

[132] *Idem*

followers of Al Qaeda in the Arabian Peninsula were instead greeted with a web page of recipes for *"The Best Cupcakes in America"*. The secretive sabotage operation was undertaken by agents at MI6 and GCHQ, the Government's listening station in Cheltenham. Both intelligence agencies have developed a variety of cyber-weapons such as computer viruses, to use against enemy states and terrorists. U.S. intelligence officials had also planned to launch a cyber-attack against the terror network after the online magazine launched, but the CIA blocked the operation, arguing that it would expose sources and methods. Al Qaeda was reportedly able to reissue the magazine two weeks later and had gone on to produce four further editions, but one source reportedly said that British intelligence was continuing to target the magazine, viewed as such a powerful propaganda tool.

4.2 The Falklands Conflict

The conflict began on Friday 2 April 1982, when Argentine forces invaded and occupied the Falkland Islands and South Georgia. The British government dispatched a naval task force to engage the Argentine Navy and Air Force, and retake the islands by amphibious assault. *"The resulting conflict lasted 74 days and ended with the Argentine surrender on 14 June 1982, which returned the islands to British control. During the conflict, 649 Argentine military personnel, 255 British military personnel and 3 Falkland Islanders died".* [133]The conflict was the result of a protracted historical confrontation regarding the sovereignty of the islands. Britain has held the South Atlantic archipelago since 1833 but Buenos Aires claims they are occupied Argentine territory.

Argentina has asserted that the Falkland Islands have been Argentine territory since the 19th century and, shows no sign of relinquishing the claim. The claim was added to the Argentine constitution after its reformation in 1994.

As such, the Argentine government characterized their initial invasion as the re-occupation of their own territory, whilst the British government saw it as an invasion of a British dependent territory.

---

[133] http://www.forces-war-records.co.uk/Information/FalklandsWarRecords

THE HISTORY OF MI6

However, neither state officially declared war and hostilities were almost exclusively limited to the territories under dispute and the local area of the South Atlantic.

During the Falklands conflict, SIS operatives were instrumental in efforts to deny the Argentineans from receiving any more of the deadly French-made Exocet missiles, several of which had already sunk British warships. Posing as arms dealers, the SIS men either bought up all the missiles available on the open and black market or posed as sellers themselves of inoperative weapons.

In his 2002 memoirs Sir John Nott, the Britain's Secretary of the State for Defense during the conflict, made the following disclosure regarding the activities of the UK's Secret Intelligence Service (MI6): *"I authorized our agents to pose as bona fide purchasers of equipment on the international market, ensuring that we outbid the Argentines, and other agents identified Exocet missiles in markets and rendered them inoperable".*[134]

4.3 Jungle operation

During the second world war, Great Britain, US and the Soviet Union were the protagonists of an unusual alliance based on circumstances and practical need rather than true friendship and cooperation. After the end of the war, (1948-1955) the western leaders found out that they have encountered a new much dangerous rival.

A gigantic nation, with large army that had seized control over all Eastern Europe, getting its grip on China and East Asia and entering the Middle East.

So British secret service SIS (MI6) and American CIA devised plans to spy on Soviet Union and attempt to sabotage it from the inside, and the occupied Baltic States was the perfect spot for such operations.

The operation was codenamed *"Jungle"*, it was a program for the clandestine insertion of intelligence and resistance agents into Poland and the Baltic states. The agents were mostly Estonian, Latvian and

---

[134] The Official History of the Falklands Campaign. War and Diplomacy by Lawrence Freedman 2005 Crown Copyright pag 386

Lithuanian refugees who had been trained in the UK and Sweden. The clandestine agent transport was organized by the British secret intelligence service MI6. The agents were transported under the cover of the "British Baltic Fishery Protection Service" (BBFPS), it was set up specifically as a cover for operation *"Jungle"*.

Commencing in May 1949," *MI6 used the Kriegsmarine Schnellboot S 208, Fast Patrol Boat or FPB, under the command of the German naval officer Hans-Helmut Klose to transport agents to the landing sites in Polanga, Lithuania, in Uzava and Ventspils, Latvia, in Saaremaa, Estonia, and in Stolpmünde, Poland".*[135] After improvised beginnings, MI6 considered a permanent organization, which was set up 1951 in Hamburg-Finkenwerder and later in Kiel. In 1952, a second Schnellboot, S 130, joined and the mission was enlarged to include signal intelligence SIGINT equipment. In 1954-1955, three newly built Schnellboote replaced the old FPBs.

From 1951 onwards, MI6 suspected that Soviet counter-intelligence might have infiltrated the spy networks in the forests of Courland. Actually, the KGB had been very successful with its "operative game" named "Lursen-S." All of the more than 42 agents which MI6 had sent were caught, sentenced, or turned around as moles or counter agents. The MI6 operations in the forests of Courland, however, were a complete failure. This had much to do with superciliousness and lack of internal security inside MI6. In the end, neither MI6 nor the KGB achieved their intended aims and many human lives were sacrificed for some information, which after close analysis proved to be without much value.

4.4 The Balkans (1990)

In the 1990s, the Balkan region was gravely affected by the wars between the former Yugoslav republics that broke out after Slovenia and Croatia held free elections and their people voted for independence on their respective countries' referendums. Serbia in turn declared

---

[135] http://latvianhistory.wordpress.com/2012/10/04/operation-jungle-the-failed-british-secret-service-mission-in-the-baltic-states-1945-1956/

the dissolution of the union as unconstitutional and the Yugoslavian army unsuccessfully tried to maintain status quo. Slovenia and Croatia declared independence on 26 June 1991, followed by the Ten-Day War in Slovenia. Till October 1991, the Army retired from Slovenia, and in Croatia, the war between the Croatian government and local Serbs would continue until 1995. In the ensuing 10 years armed confrontation, gradually all the other Republics declared independence, with Bosnia being the most affected by the fighting.

The long lasting wars resulted in a United Nations intervention and NATO ground and air forces took action against Serb forces in Bosnia and Herzegovina and Serbia, including its southern province of Kosovo.

From the dissolution of Yugoslavia six republics achieved international recognition as sovereign republics: Slovenia, Croatia, Bosnia and Herzegovina, Macedonia, Montenegro and Serbia.

SIS operations in the former Yugoslavia include the hunting down war criminals, the organization also developed contacts within the various factions in the region and facilitated local peace deals.

"It has long been rumoured that the SIS had plans to assassinate the Serb leader, Slobodan Milosevic, by blinding his car's driver with a special flash-gun built into a camera".[136]

4.5 Operation Mass Appeal

The British MI6 establishes Operation Mass Appeal, a British intelligence mission designed to exaggerate the threat of Iraq's alleged arsenal of weapons of mass destruction in order to shape public opinion.

The operation plants stories in the domestic and foreign media from the 1990s through 2003. Intelligence used by Mass Appeal was defined as *"single source data of dubious quality"*.[137] After the First Gulf War, the operation seeks to justify the UN sanctions policy. But after the September 11 attacks, its objective is to secure public support for an invasion of Iraq.

---

[136] http://www.eliteukforces.info/mi6/
[137] https://www.fas.org/irp/eprint/leitenberg3.html

The government confirmed that MI6 had organized *"Operation Mass Appeal"*, a campaign to plant stories in the media about Saddam Hussein's weapons of mass destruction. The revelation of the so much discussed *"dodgy dossier"* [138], created embarrassing questions for Tony Blair in the run-up to the publication of the report by Lord Hutton and, in the circumstances surrounding the death of Dr David Kelly, the government weapons expert.

The aim was to convince the public that Iraq was a far greater threat than it actually was.

Blair justified his backing for sanctions and for the invasion of Iraq on the grounds that intelligence reports showed Saddam was working to acquire chemical, biological and nuclear weapons.

During the first gulf war, 1991, the SIS were involved with stirring up an unsuccessful Kurdish rebellion against Saddam Hussein's regime. While in 2003, during the second Gulf War, with UK forces SIS approached from the South, SIS were active inside the southern Iraqi city of Basra, creating a network of agents in preparation for the invasion.

SIS also assisted the *"SBS"*[139] in gathering intelligence that aided the UK's entry into the city. They ran agents, snatched prisoners and identified targets for air strikes. In post invasion Basra, the SIS provided

---

[138] Also known as the September Dossier, was a document published by the British government on 24 September 2002 on the same day of a recall of Parliament to discuss the contents of the document. The paper was part of an ongoing investigation by the government into weapons of mass destruction in Iraq, which ultimately led to the 2003 invasion of Iraq. It contained a number of false allegations according to which Iraq also possessed weapons of mass destruction, including chemical weapons and biological weapons. The dossier even alleged that Iraq had reconstituted its nuclear weapons program.

[139] http://www.eliteukforces.info/mi6/
The Special Boat Service (SBS) is the special forces unit of the Royal Navy.
The SBS can trace their origins to the Second World War, when they were formed as the Special Boat Section in 1940. They became the Special Boat Squadron after the Second World War and the Special Boat Service in the 1980s.

intel for the SBS in its efforts to track down members of the Baath regime.

In one such incident, the SBS called in an air strike on a house that the SIS had identified as the location of Ali Hassan al-Majid, otherwise known as "Chemical Ali", a most-wanted member of Saddam's regime. Due to communication problems, the raid was not a success, however other air strikes called in by SIS and SBS teams were successful.

4.6 Operation Ajax

The 1953 Iranian coup d'état was the Western-led covert operation that deposed the democratically elected government of Iranian Prime Minister Mohammad Mossadegh. The coup was organized by the United States' CIA and the United Kingdom's MI6, who aided abetted anti Mossadegh royalists and mutinous Iranian Army officers in overthrowing the Prime Minister.

"President Eisenhower authorized the CIA officer Kermit Roosevelt Jr. in conjunction with MI6, to carry out Operation Ajax"[140] to aid retired General Fazlollah Zahedi and Imperial Guard Colonel Nemotllah Nassiri to establish a pro US and pro UK government, by corrupting Iranian government officials, reporters, and business men.

This Anglo American coup d'état was to ensure Western control of Iran's petroleum and to prevent Eastern USSR hegemony upon Iran.

Moreover, the Iranian motivations for deposing PM Mossadegh included reactionary clerical dissatisfaction with a secular government, fomented with CIA propaganda.

The decision was made in June 1953 Dr. Mohammad Mossadegh had to replace with General Fazlollah Zahedi ; one of those arrested in February 1953 on charges of plotting to overthrow the nationalist government.

Kermit Roosevelt, the CIA Mideast Agent, traveled secretly to Iran to coordinate the Operation Ajax with the Shah and the Iranian military, which was led by General Fazlollah Zahedi.

---

[140] Operation AJAX; Roots of a Tree Grown in Distrust, 2012 pag 1

In accordance with the plan, on August 16, 1953, the Shah violated the Iran's Monarchy Constitution and dismissed Dr. Mossadegh and his nationalist cabinet without the parliament's approval and appointed General Fazlollah Zahedi as the new Prime Minister.

The chief of the Royal Guards, Colonel Nematollah Nassiri, served Dr. Mossadegh with a formal dismissal notice. In addition, he was ordered to occupy Dr. Mossadegh's house by the Royal troops and hold him in his house until further instructions, but the Prime Minister's guards forced them to quit.

The coup d'état was publicized and caused major disappointment and dissatisfaction amongst the people throughout the country. In a matter of hours, massive rioting erupted in Iran in wide support of Dr. Mossadegh; and the Shah fled to Italy. The people's protest and demonstration continued for two days and led to pull down the statues of the Shah and his father all over the country.

On August 19th, 1953, the British Intelligence Service (MI6) and the United States Central Intelligence Agency (CIA), engineered to perform the next phase of their plan against the Iranian national government of Dr. Mossadegh. On that day, a group of tanks led by General Fazlollah Zahedi moved through Tehran and surrounded Dr. Mossadegh's residence. The forces behind the coup d'état also managed to pull a large number of bribed hooligans into the streets to rally against Dr. Mossadegh. Finally the army and police forces let the crowd reach the Prime Minister's residence and after hours of bombarding and fighting a bloody battle with the small group of Dr. Mossadegh's loyal guards, they entered the house and after plundering it, they burned it down. In a few time Dr. Mossadegh and his top cabinet leaders surrendered themselves to the coup d'état Prime Minister, General Fazlollah Zahedi.

Dr. Mossadegh remains a great figure in the history of modern Iran. As an individual he had a reputation for honesty, integrity, and sincerity. He strongly opposed British and, later, American influence in Iran. He was an eloquent, impassioned orator, and his speeches are still widely read in Iran.

During Dr. Mossadegh's trial in the Shah's military court, he publicized the secrets of two military coup d'état attempts against his government. He was sentenced to three years imprisonment; thereafter he was transferred to his country house in Ahmad-Abad at the age of 74 and lived there under house arrest until his death. On March 4, 1967, Dr. Mossadegh died of cancer at the age of 84.

The Iranian people never forgave the Shah for the 1953 illegitimate and bloody coup d'état against the Iranian national hero, Dr. Mohammad Mossadegh and his nationalist cabinet.

The Iranian people deeply suffered under the Shah's dictatorship, corruption, phony elections, heavy censorship on the public media, torture and execution of thousands of dissenters until the 1979 Revolution.

Altough now judged a fiasco, the Eisenhower Administration originally championed Operation Ajax and considered it a triumphant secret war.

4.7 Pakistan Operation

One special operation by MI6 in Pakistan, *"named MI6's Pakistan Operation"*[141], revealed a major terror attack being planned in Britain. The major investigations by the MI6 officers and secret agents revealed the possibilities of links between some of the Al-Qaeda commanders in Pakistan and some people in U.K.

"The UKs top intelligence agency, MI6, financed terror attacks in Pakistan through Al-Qaeda operative by paying him at least $ 100,000 per month, it has been reliably learnt".[142]

The sponsorship helped Al-Qaeda carry out bombing on the French submarine engineers in Karachi and churches in rural Punjab, which left several woman and children dead.

Sources also revealed that the MI6 had 'conveyed to the UK leadership that the Al-Qaeda operative Adil Hadi al Jazairi Bin Hamlili 'misused the funds and carried out terror attacks inside Pakistan. The British intelligence agency also informed their government that they were innocent and had no idea that the cash, they were paying to the agent, would be used to kill French engineers and Pakistani civilians, according to a diplomatic source.

---

[141] http://www.guardian.co.uk/uk/2009/apr/11/terrorism-intelligence-pakistan
[142] http://www.historycommons.org/entity.jsp?entity=uk_secret_intelligence_service

Sources also said that the British government has mulled holding of judicial inquiry to be headed by a former Court of Appeal judge who monitors the intelligence agencies for the government after MI6 found involved in openly funding to terrorists in the name of informants operations.

The disclosure that MI6 funded terror attacks on French submarine engineers in Karachi and churches in rural Punjab has sparked anger in France and Pakistan, diplomatic sources said, adding, the incident also links British spy network with terrorist outfits. *"The Al-Qaeda operative accused of bombing two Christian churches and a luxury hotel in Pakistan in 2002 was at the same time working for British intelligence, according to secret files on detainees who were shipped to the US military's Guantanamo Bay prison camp".*[143]

Hamlili had provided little intelligence input to MI6 about Al-Qaedas operations in UK and they (MI6-men) rewarded him with 0.5 million US dollars. This huge cash helped him plan, finance and carry out bombing outside Karachi's Sheraton hotel in May 2002 that killed 11 French submarine engineers and two Pakistanis.

The US intelligence reports also confirmed that Adil Hadi al Jazairi Bin Hamlili, an Algerian citizen, was involved in a bombing outside Karachi's Sheraton hotel in 2002. According to the files, Hamlili told his American interrogators at Bagram that he had been running a carpet business from Peshawar.

But his CIA captors knew the Algerian had been an informant for MI6 and Canada's Secret Intelligence Service for over three years and suspected he had been double-crossing handlers. According to US intelligence the two spy agencies recruited Hamlili as a "humint" human intelligence source in December 2000 "because of his connections to members of various Al-Qaida linked groups that operated in Afghanistan and Pakistan."

It is well also to underline that the UKs top intelligence agency became a laughing stock worldwide for paying hefty amount to a Taliban impostor in an attempt to broker a deal between the NATO forces and the Afghan Taliban.

---

[143] http://socioecohistory.wordpress.com/2011/04/27/guantanamo-bay-al-qaida-terrorist-assassin-worked-for-mi6/

4.8 Operation Victory

Since its existence, the MI6 has been known to put to task many foreign operations out, of which some have gained laurels and some have gained criticism.

"Operation Victory" is the example of an operation that did not meet the desired results and finally the court embarrassed the MI6's operations in contrast with the investigation ethics and the rules of the courts.

"An MI6 agent (Brian Gibbs) has been accused of wrecking a £15m money laundering trial in the Cayman Islands by destroying crucial evidence on the instructions of his handlers in London". [144]

Cayman Islands, a sort of tax even in the Caribbean, between Jamaica and Cuba, very close to the drug barons and tax dodgers of Miami. The

islands' lucrative off shore industry has made them a magnet for organized crime. They claim to be the world's fifth largest financial centre.

However, the Caymans spent some time on an international blacklist imposed by the anti money laundering organization Financial Action Task Force.

Britain, the colonial power, has come under pressure to clean up the islands. And since the end of the cold war MI6 itself has found a new role gathering intelligence on drug runners, organized crime and money launderers.

The famous story of collapse of a major trial and the subsequent exposure of MI6's operations shows, how difficult is for the secret service to find and reconcile intelligence gathering with law enforcement.

MI6 tried to hide its true role during the prolonged trial, but the attempt failed.

Everything started in 1999, when a US arrest led the Cayman's UK-appointed governor to close one of the local banks, the Euro Bank Corporation.

"A bank client, Kenneth Taves, had been arrested in California and charged with masterminding a $25m credit card fraud". [145]

---

[144] http://www.thesundaytimes.co.uk/sto/news/uk_news/article215808.ece
[145] http://www.guardian.co.uk/uk

Investigations began into alleged personal payments he had been making to a British banker in the Caymans.

A former Metropolitan Police detective, Brian Gibbs, director of Cayfin, the Cayman Islands' financial reporting unit, played a key role in the investigations. But, unknown to many on the island, he was also working for MI6.

In 2000 the Cayman authorities laid charges against nine people connected to the Euro Bank scandal. Four people still on the islands were brought to trial, Brian Cunha, Judith Donegan, Ivan Burges and Donald Stewart, who are all believed to be British expatriates.

But when the trial began a valid team began to investigate the background of prosecution witness Edward Warwick, a Euro Bank assistant manager.

It was unearthed his role as an informant to the head of Cayfin, in a trail that eventually led to MI6. Mr Brian Gibbs was forced to disclose some of his links and his mole was revealed.

To help their man out of the crisis, MI6 constructed an elaborate scheme to return a censored version of the records Mr Gibbs had originally sent to London. This could be produced as though it was a genuine Cayfin document.

The plan didn't work. The records were contradictory and the deception unravelled.

An MI6 controller was eventually forced to testify to the Cayman court under the pseudonym *"John Doe"* [146]and *"conceded Mr Gibbs had destroyed evidence completely and unquestioningly on MI6 orders"*.[147]

The judge decided to rule that efforts by Mr Gibbs and MI6 to hide the intelligence files fatally prejudiced the case against the Euro Bank defendants.

---

[146] Name used when the true identity is unknown
[147] http://www.guardian.co.uk/uk/2003/jan/18/military1

CONCLUSIONS

Finally, SIS or to use its more popular name MI6, is responsible of all overseas espionage activities related to British security. The task of the Secret Intelligence Service, is to study, discover and steal the secrets of others. At the same time it has always tried to protect its own.

For most part of its existence, secrecy was so important that MI6 did not even exist. At least not officially. The outside world never knew its name, its operations, its collectors.

But that era has passed, consequently, the modern world and the threats posed by it ask greater accountability and transparency and cautiously, the Secret Service came out of the closet.

This research is an attempt to understand the wider issues surrounding British intelligence and the historical evolution of a particularly organization that the time has transformed.

The first part introduces the origin and the role of MI6. Its birth due to an increasingly threatening Germany, its difficulties and successes during the two World Wars, the Cold War and the KGB. Also shows the parallel growth shared with the domestic security agency MI5 and the valuable collaboration with the American CIA.

The aim of the second part is to describe how the agency works today with the cooperation of the British Intelligence Community.

The following part focuses on the work and functions of fifteen presidents who have been directed the agency from the foundation of the organization to the present day. From the first eccentric head Mansfield Smith-Cumming to the current *"C"* John Sawers, reporting the main actions of each in the framework of the global issues and crises that accompanied their term in office. And at the end, just some of the numerous operations in which SIS was participant are reported, emphasizing both triumphs and disasters because not always SIS operation has given the desired results.

BIBLIOGRAPHY

ALDRICH R., *CGHQ The uncensored story of Britain's most secret intelligence,* Harper Collins publisher 2010

Andrew C. M., *At her majesty's secret service—The Chiefs of Britain's Intelligence Agency, MI6,* Greenhill books, london 2006

Andrew C., NOAKES J., *Intelligence And International Relations, 1900-1945,* Liverpool University Press 1987

BAMFORD J., BENNET R.M., *Espionage: Spies and Secrets*—Virgin 2003

BENNET RICHARD M. *A Short History of the British Secret Intelligence Service, MI-6*

Davies P. H. J., *MI6 and the machinery of spying,* Frank Cass Publisher, London 2004 de Santis S., *Spionaggio nella Seconda Guerra Mondiale,* Giunti editore, Firenze 2001

Dorril S., *MI6: Inside the Covert World of Her Majesty's Secret Intelligence Service,* Simon & Schuster, London 2002

Dorril S., *MI6: Fifty years of special operations,* Fourth Estate Ltd 2001

ELLIOTT M. THOMAS R., *Public law* Oxford University Press 2008

FREEDMAN L. *The Official History of the Falklands Campaign. War and Diplomacy,* Crown Copyright 2005

HAYNES A., *Invisible Power: The Elizabethan Secret Services 1570-1603* Sutton Publishing Ltd, 1992

Jeffrey K., *MI6—The secret history of the secret intelligence service,* Bloomsbury, London 2010

Jeffrey K., *The secret history of MI6: 1909-1949,* Penguin Group, London 2010

JEFFREY RICHELSON T., *A Century of Spies: Intelligence in the Twentieth Century,* University Press 1997

Kelly S., Gorst A., *Whitehall and the Suez Crisis,* Frank Cass publisher, London 2000

King J., Beveridge J., *Princess Diana—the hidden evidence*, S.P.I. Books, London 2001

Knightely P., *The Second Oldest Profession: The Spy As Bureaucrat, Patriot, Fantasist and Whore*, Deustch publisher, London 1986

MATHERLY CARTER, *Operation AJAX, Roots of a Tree Grown in Distrust*

McCormack S., *Inside Britain's MI6: Military Intelligence 6*, Rosen Publishing Group, New York 2003

STANIFORTH A. SAMPSON F., *The Routledge Companion to UK Counter-Terrorism,* Routledge 2012

Smith M., *MI6: the real James Bond 1909-1939*, Dialogue publishing, 2011

TRAHAIR R.C.S., *Encyclopedia of Cold War Espionage, Spies, and Secret Operations,* Greenwood publishing group 2004

TOMLINSON R. DAVIES B., *The Spycraft Manual: The Insider's Guide to Espionage Techniques,* Zenith Imprint 2005

Thomas G., *Secret wars: one hundred years of British intelligence inside MI5 and MI6*, St. Martin's Press, London 2010

WADHAM J., *The Intelligence service act 1994" The Modern Law Vol. 57* Review Limited 1994

WARNER KLIMCZUK S., *Secret Places, Hidden Sanctuaries: Uncovering Mysterious Sites, Symbols, and societies,* Sterling publication 2009

West N., *MI6: British Intelligence service operations, 1909-45*, Random House, London 1983

WEB SOURCES

https://www.sis.gov.uk/
http://www.nationalarchives.gov.uk/pathways/firstworldwar/first_world_war/origins_conflict.htm
http://www.mathaba.net/data/sis/history.shtml
http://www.andrewwilliams.tv/books/the-poison-tide/secret-service/
http://www.faqs.org/espionage/Lo-Mo/MI6-British-Secret-Intelligence-Service.html
http://www.independent.co.uk/news/uk/this-britain/mi6-building-is-rocked-by-two-explosions-698855.html
http://en.wikipedia.org/wiki/Secret_Intelligence_Service
http://www.historytoday.com/blog/2012/05/mi6-history-secret-intelligence-service
http://www.mi5.com/security/mi6org/index.htm
http://www.magnacartaplus.org/bills/rip/index.htm
http://www.eliteukforces.info/mi6/
http://www.inside-news.ch/shayler/ukb.htm
http://www.fantompowa.net/Flame/diana_tomlinson.htm
http://www.zrs.upr.si/media/uploads/files/bajc
http://www.guardian.co.uk/uk/mi6
http://www.telegraph.co.uk/news/ uknews/terrorism-in-the-uk/MI6.html
http://www.britannica.com/search?query=mi6
http://www.guardian.co.uk/uk/2009/apr/11/terrorism-intelligence-pakistan
http: //top-topics.thefullwiki.org/Chiefs_of_MI6
http://www.faqs.org /espionage
https:/ /www.mi5.gov.uk/careers/working-at-mi5/working-with-mi6-and-gchq/mi5-or-mi6.aspx
http:/ /www.gchq.gov.uk/Pages/homepage.aspx
http://news.bbc.co.uk/2/hi/uk_news/politics/286128.stm

http://www.sourcewatch.org/index.php/Front_groups
http:/ /usatoday30.usatoday.com/news/world/story/2012-04-29/bin-laden-anniversary/54630274/1
http://archive.is/HyDm
http:/ /isc.independent.gov.uk/
http://www.spartacus.schoolnet.co.uk/FWWm6.htm
http://www.forces-war-records.co.uk/Information/FalklandsWarRecords
http://latvianhistory.wordpress.com/2012/10/04/operation-jungle-the-failed-british-secret-service-mission-in-the-baltic-states-1945-1956/
https://www.fas.org/irp/eprint/leitenberg3.htm
http://www.historycommons.org/entity.jsp?entity=uk_secret_intelligence_service
http://socioecohistory.wordpress.com/2011/04/27/guantanamo-bay-al-qaida-terrorist-assassin-worked-for-mi6/
http://www.thesundaytimes.co.uk/sto/news/uk_news/article215808.ece